D1029845

"How stocks are valued is a core question for econo-mists, policymakers, and investors. Kevin Hassett's highly readable book translates insights from research on assett pricing to bridge the divide between academic and popular discussions of 'bubbles.' In addition, the book's clever and understandable discussion of effects of uncertainty on valuation is well worth the read."

> — GLENN HUBBARD, the Russell L. Carson Professor at Columbia Business School and professor of economics in the Faculty of Arts and Sciences at Columbia University

"Kevin Hassett has a remarkable capacity for making complicated ideas accessible. His lively writing in *Bubbleology* brings deep insights to bear on important questions of interest to finance professionals and individual investors, and in the most entertaining way imaginable."

> — CHARLES W. CALOMIRIS, the Paul M. Montrone Professor of Finance and Economics, Columbia Business School.

BUBBLEOLOGY

THE NEW SCIENCE OF STOCK MARKET
WINNERS AND LOSERS

KEVIN HASSETT

A CROWN BUSINESS
BRIEFINGS BOOK

CROWN
BUSINESS
NEW YORK

Published by Crown Business, New York, New York.
Member of the Crown Publishing Group, a division of Random
House, Inc.
www.randomhouse.com

CROWN BUSINESS is a trademark and the Rising Sun colophon is
a registered trademark of Random House, Inc.

Printed in the United States of America

Design by Meryl Sussman Levavi / Digitext

Library of Congress Cataloging-in-Publication Data
Hassett, Kevin A.
    Bubbleology: the amazing science of stock market bubbles/
    by Kevin Hassett.—1st ed.
      p.   cm.—(Crown business briefings book)
    Includes bibliographical references.
    1. Stocks—Prices.   2. Speculation.   3. Investment analysis.
    I. Title.   II. Series.

  HG4636.H32 2002
  332.63'222—dc21   2002023386

ISBN 0-609-60929-7

10 9 8 7 6 5 4 3 2 1

First Edition

For my family: John, James, and Kristie Hassett

Contents

BUBBLEOLOGY

Preface

When stock prices soar, investors are confronted with two competing pieces of conventional wisdom. One comes from a media that always makes bad news out of good. Higher prices signal a "speculative bubble," and the forward-looking implication is clear: Soon the bubble will pop and only a fool would stay in the market. On the other hand, investment professionals—many of whom have been trained in our top business schools—tell us not to worry. The market always works. Higher prices reflect the wisdom of the omnipotent market gods. Question the market and you are committing blasphemy. Investors are assured that if they repeat the holy mantra "buy and hold," everything will turn out fine.

Both cannot be right. Deciding whom to believe is one of the most important choices that we make. Yet there is so little to go on if one relies upon the popular debate. Most of all, the motives of these debaters are highly suspicious. Many who claim to see bubbles desperately believe that the capitalist system itself cannot be trusted, and secretly hope it will fail. Defenders of the market are often those who will profit the most if an investor decides to buy stocks.

Who should be believed? Is there a way for investors to evaluate price increases and price declines and identify whether they are happening for good or bad reasons? Is there a way of thinking about stocks that would have enabled investors to profit successfully from stock market investments without exposing their fortunes to the risk of extreme calamities like the collapse of the Internet sector? These are the questions that motivated the writing of this book.

The questions come up almost every day. In October 2001, for example, the share price for Yahoo!, the Internet search engine, doubled. Did the price rise for good reasons, or was another bubble forming?

Now, more than ever, the answers are within our grasp. A few simple tools can help the prudent investor separate the wheat from the chaff and avoid investing in sectors or shares that are more likely to be affected by a bubble.

The book relies upon a large but recent scientific literature. While the angry partisans have debated bubbles in the popular press, a quiet revolution has been brewing below the surface. Feisty scholars from many different fields have spent the past decade developing new tools for the analysis of stock markets, and the fruits of those efforts are bountiful. This work has mostly stayed out of the public eye, buried in technical papers with more equations than words. Some of the best work has even been done by physicists. Yet the information contained in these dusty journals is invaluable to investors, and surprisingly easy to turn to practical use.

In the pages that follow, this new work will be described in detail, and its lessons will be used to assess the popular conventional wisdom. While *both* of the traditional schools cannot be right, the real surprise that follows from the latest findings is that *neither* is. Instead, three themes emerge that are crucial to a practical understanding of how the market works.

Pessimists Often Cry Wolf, but Sometimes a Wolf Is There

As the dot-com prices were increasing, many thought that the parallels to earlier crazes were eerie. Anatol Kaletsky captured a common theme in the London *Times* in early 1999 when he wrote, "The present speculation in Internet shares bears all the hallmarks of a financial bubble. The Internet frenzy may not be quite as bizarre as Tulipmania, when people made and lost fortunes buying Dutch tulip bulbs with no practical use apart from their ability to create more tulips. But the Internet does bear comparison with the South Sea Bubble as well as the speculation in railway shares in the mid-19th century."

The earliest anecdotal example cited by Kaletsky was the Dutch Tulipmania of the mid 1630s. This episode was etched into the American consciousness by wealthy financier—and economic adviser to presidents—Bernard Baruch. In 1934, Baruch wrote, in an introduction to Charles Mackay's classic treatise *Extraordinary Popular Delusions and the Madness of Crowds*, that Mackay's detailed description of the Dutch Tulipmania had saved him his fortune. Recognizing the repetition of behavior documented by Mackay, Baruch bailed out of the market just before the Great Crash. Mackay's thesis was that a kind of madness could sweep over a crowd, leading to chimerical financial events. Sixty-five years later, appeal to it may have saved Kaletsky's readers their own fortunes.

Crazy things do happen. The awe-inspiring surge and drop in Internet share prices was clearly a strange event that is difficult to reconcile with the view that share prices are always right. During the surge, many Wall Street firms aggressively advised their clients to purchase high-tech stocks. In part, this may have reflected a religious faith in markets—they continued to sing the same old song, and failed to acquire a healthy wariness of the skyrocketing prices. It may also reflect a conflict of interest. However, one can forgive their clients for listening to this advice. The bears were also singing their same old song. Many of those who most presciently warned against dot-com stocks previously warned against the dangers of stock ownership. Listening to this advice has been very unprofitable. An investor who invested $2,000 in the stock market in 1950 saw her stake grow to $1.2 million by 2001. An investor who listened to the bears throughout and invested in bonds saw her stake grow to a paltry $25,000.

So the bears may be on to something, but they are often wrong. Recently, researchers have discovered that the times that they are right have something in common.

Traditional Risk Measures Are Almost Worthless

Why do the market students with lofty academic credentials have so much trouble with unusual events, and even appear less successful at times to capture market conceptual trends than financial journalists? The best explanation is that their scientific methods were admirable, but the models they rely upon to understand the world are flawed. This has become especially apparent in recent years, as researchers at the frontier have developed new, more effective models to replace the old ones still relied upon by financial advisers.

The key insight of these new models is that the old way of evaluating risk is inherently flawed and incomplete. Modern financial analysis was developed by men and women who believed that risk is the same thing as volatility. If a share price fluctuated a whole lot in the past, then that share is very risky. If the price was stable in the past, then that stock is not risky. This simple assumption was very powerful. It allowed financial professionals to develop a tremendously impressive artifice that relied upon lessons from centuries of mathematical research analyzing random events. Buying a stock is, according to this view, like wagering on coin flips. Understand the mathematics of coin flips, and you can comprehend the complex world of financial markets.

We have now learned that this approach is misguided. While such volatility is symptomatic of risk, it is hardly the only consideration. A much more risky circumstance is one in which a firm is venturing out into a new area that has never been explored before. When you flip a coin, there is a 50 percent chance that you get heads or tails. If you are deciding to gamble on a coin flip, it is easy to figure out the possible outcomes. But when a firm is trying something completely new, something that may fundamentally alter the economic landscape, there are no probabilities. Nobody knows for sure what might happen. For such a firm, circumstances are too ambiguous to be analyzed using the approach recommended by financial professionals. Sensible investors must decide what to buy and what to sell armed with little history to go on. How can the market find the perfect price, the "right answer" in such circumstances, when no logically correct answer exists? At that point, the market is asked to achieve the impossible, and it is there that the most promising evidence of bubbles lurks.

The Market Is Brilliant, but Not Perfect

Sometimes it is easy to figure out what something should be worth. Sometimes it is difficult. Occasionally, it is almost impossible. The stock market sets the prices of shares every day, regardless of how easy or hard that might be. When millions of investors trade shares between themselves each day, the price that results reflects an awe-inspiring collective wisdom. When somebody steps forward and cries that the market is too high or too low, he or she makes a claim to superior knowledge that more often than not has been proven wrong.

In the television series *Star Trek: The Next Generation,* a foe more horrible than any ever encountered by the earthlings and their United Federation of Planets was introduced. The Borg were an alien species of cyborgs—half human and half machine. Their biological brains were interlaced by an enormous wireless Internet. Each member of "the collective" accessed the thoughts and knowledge of all of the other members. This connectedness made the race superrational. The technologies that the collective devised were far more advanced than those developed by the humans and their allies.

A vast integration of the knowledge of millions of beings is indeed a formidable concept, and it is perhaps the best surviving description of the stock market. The market often performs feats of valuation that turn out, in retrospective, to have been strikingly insightful. It is most often the case that things that appear strange turn out to have been sensible under the circumstances. They appeared strange at the time only because the intelligence of an individual is much less potent than the intelligence of the collective. Thus, one should be especially wary of claims that a bubble is present, that the market is all wrong. This has often been true of events that became bubble legends. Charles Mackay's thesis, for example, has been studied extensively in recent years, and it has not stood up well to close scrutiny. The mighty Tulipmania itself may not have been as crazy as Mackay described it.

In many ways, that is a shame. It would have been fortuitous if Mackay had been proven correct and bubble phenomena in the past were attributable to hysteria. The problem would be that much easier to understand and cure. A collective trip to the psychiatrist and a couple of pills might end bubbles once and for all. While there are many surprises in the following pages, perhaps the greatest is this: The individual human behavior that has been observed in many apparent manias may well be rational under the circumstances, even if the result of that behavior—wild swings in prices—appears not to be. This has enormous significance. Individuals often try not to repeat their mistakes, and they try to cure themselves of their psychological inadequacies. If the latest and most fascinating bubble research is correct, bubbles may exist but not be caused by mistakes at all. Instead, people use tools that have been honed over the millennia by evolution to do the best they can when they have very little information to go on—when risks that are ignored by traditional measures are especially high.

Such circumstances are an indelible part of life, which suggests that even if the events surrounding the bubbles of history are carefully documented, and their study required reading for all market participants, we nonetheless could expect something like the financial events of 1999 and 2000 to recur again and again. Accordingly, what follows may be something more than an intellectual diversion.

CHAPTER ONE

Bubbles, Markets, and Frontiers

There are many questions that vex people who study the economy and financial markets. However, the one that uses up the most brainpower is the question of whether financial bubbles exist. A *financial bubble* is a period when the price of an asset (stocks, real estate, tulips, etc.) suddenly soars for irrational reasons and then collapses. The search is difficult for a simple reason. Price increases are not always bad. Shares of the major pharmaceutical company Amgen, for example, soared more than 1,000 percent in the 1990s as the firm matured from a promising start-up to a profit-making giant. Such an increase made sense given the enormous success of Amgen's drug-development team. Sometimes stock prices soar and stay high. Sometimes, like the Internet-based stocks, they crash back to earth. It is easy, after the fact, to say that a bubble popped.

The question of whether an asset is increasing in price based on a solid foundation or a chimera is important. Far too many people excuse themselves from participating in the stock market because of an irrational fear of rising prices. These fears are fueled by pundits who abhor every price increase. Sometimes they are right, but often they are not.

For some the search for bubbles has a purely intellectual motivation. Others correctly recognize the tremendous financial potential of a reliable bubble indicator. If you get in on the bubble early and get out just in time, you can make a fortune. Many researchers discussed in this book have devoted themselves to the struggle of defining and discovering bubbles with the focus and the energy that accompanied classic philosophical explorations of far deeper questions. With apologies to the sages, the view of the world emerging from the work on bubbles is at times just as exhilarating as the work of the great philosophers. The search for bubbles has uncovered much more than a window to a quick financial killing.

Because of the possible financial gain, the search for bubbles has been around for centuries, and it has frustrated scientists for just as long. Sir Isaac Newton remarked once, after witnessing the puzzling financial swings of his time, that "I can calculate the motion of heavenly bodies, but not the madness of people." Economists began trying to do the latter in the late 1970s, but today they are not alone. As the problems involved in detecting stock market bubbles have become well known, scientists from other disciplines, including psychology, evolutionary biology, mathematics, and theoretical physics, have joined the hunt. Together these men and women have developed a framework that provides a picture of the breeding ground for bubbles. That foundation has helped us understand why bubbles might occur, and, as important, it has provided a new context for organizing our perceptions about the structure of our everyday lives.

What have they learned? The biggest success is that researchers are now asking the right questions. In the hope of getting money out before a financial bubble pops, investors have always wanted to know when a bubble might occur. But far more interesting, it turns out, is the investigation of *where* they occur. What nooks of the economy are most prone to bubbles? How can the ways people think and interact in specific environments create situations in which strange events can happen?

The search for answers to these questions has been pursued with a heightened sense of urgency in recent years. This is partly because progress has motivated extra effort, but the ideological stakes are high as well. When philosopher Adam Smith wrote *The Wealth of Nations* in 1776, he laid out a conceptual framework that correctly (at least up to now) predicted the triumph of capitalism. According to Smith, the natural functioning of a free-market system sets prices more efficiently than any other mechanism. How much should an apple cost? By matching supply and demand, the market, as if guided by an invisible hand, finds the right price. When markets function well, the price of everything—even the price of a stock—is set rationally, as if by a giant computer. Almost two hundred years after *The Wealth of Nations,* Friedrich A. Hayek, Nobel-winning economist and architect of the famed Austrian School of economists, presciently argued that Smith's work implied the certain failure of centrally planned economies. With the fall of the Soviet Union, the view that free markets work seemingly triumphed.

STABILITY OR LUCK?

But while history was siding with Smith, a nagging concern has dogged the theoreticians who sought to replace philosophical argument with rigorous mathematical proofs. The conclusion that "free markets always work" was not as robust as many expected. It applied to a very narrow set of unrealistic circumstances. As work progressed, it became increasingly difficult to defend the view that markets were necessarily highly efficient. This was especially true when economists turned to the study of financial markets.

The failure of theory to provide firm conclusions about the stability and the efficiency of financial markets haunted researchers for another reason. Everyday experience often seemed to challenge the view that markets are perfect. Prices for financial assets were prone to sudden and mysterious swings. Crowds of investors bought in a frenzy, drove prices higher, and then stampeded out in panic moments later. It is impossible to overstate how profoundly those facts have disturbed free-market thinkers. If Smith's theory could not be shown to apply to financial markets and if quirky and irrational financial booms and panics occurred fairly regularly, perhaps his entire framework might ultimately be rejected. Since financial markets are crucial to all markets, perhaps Smith was wrong about everything. Free-market economies may have won the Cold War because of nothing more than dumb luck.

While the issues involved are complex, the conceptual problem is quite straightforward. Each of us faces it every day. Let's start with a simple example. A fairly rudimentary mechanism sets the price of apples. Folks hungry for apples show up at the farmers' market, and a farmer shows up with bushels of apples. One side knows what it wants, and the other side knows what it has. A price naturally and efficiently follows. If the market will close in an hour and the farmer has many apples left, he lowers his price. If a crowd of hungry apple enthusiasts storms the farmer's apple cart and he sells everything in a few minutes, he might decide to charge a higher price tomorrow. There is no reason to believe that the price resulting from such a process is wrong.

But the game is much trickier for financial assets. A stock pays a dividend today and will likely again. How much people should be willing to pay for that stock depends on how they view the future of the company. If investors think that the company will be bankrupt next year, then they should sell the stock today. If they think that the company will develop a cure for cancer next year, then they will buy stock quickly. Since the value of such assets depends on what people believe about the future, rather than how hungry they know themselves to be today, the possibility arises that incorrect or irrational beliefs could influence prices. Everything depends on what we believe about the future, but what do we believe? Why do we believe it? Under what circumstances does the past provide a useful bellwether for the future? When are we clueless? One cannot understand bubbles without knowing the answers to these questions.

Answers can crop up unexpectedly, even in ancient history.

THE SUMERIANS AND US

Early in the seventeenth century, German scholar Englebert
Kaempfer began the arduous task of decoding the ancient
Sumerian written language that he dubbed *cuneiform.*
Various wedge-shaped inscriptions had survived on stone
ruins in Persia, as had clay tablets with engravings remi-
niscent of a drunken bird's haphazard footprints.

Some tablets have been dated back to 4000 B.C. In
addition to shedding light on the language of the ancient
Sumerians, the tablets have provided modern scholars
with a surprisingly nuanced picture of their history and
their economics. Why economics? Six thousand years ago
committing something to written form was difficult. A
scribe might well have been hired for a handsome fee. He
would delicately chip away at a stone tablet to create the
desired inscription. What was so important that it justified
such an investment? A contract!

The Sumerian contracts provide a wealth of fascinating information about those great people. Farmers would
agree to trade a certain amount of corn for silver. Most
interesting, the trades were not always immediate—the
ancients created crude futures markets. A typical contract
might require that a farmer pay a different amount to a
lender depending on the success of his crop.

The lives of these men and women were much like
our own. They struggled with the exigencies of each day
but also worried about the future. Then, as now, people
tried to look ahead and often used intuitive expectations
to design their agreements. If I have ten ears of corn and
you have a bag of wheat flour today, we can easily come
to agreement about the terms of trade. But how much is a

bag of wheat worth when delivered in six months? Clearly the answer depends on what we expect to happen between now and then. If the Hittites march through and devour our crops, a bag of wheat six months from now will be more precious than life itself. If the summer is peaceful and rainy, the crop will be bountiful, and a bag of wheat will be almost worthless. So what is the right price? Then, as now, no precise answer existed. Traders used their gut feelings to do their best.

Early Sumerian society, initially bounded by the Tigris and the Euphrates Rivers, gradually spread from a well-defined interior to a fuzzy frontier. At the frontier, citizens lived close to peoples of different cultures. Villagers at the edge faced the risk of being attacked by invaders, plundered by thieves, or eaten by wild animals. In the interior, man's control over the military and environments was more secure. Forts and walls defended strategic points. Intricate ditch systems helped protect crops and people from floods.

For our purposes, what is most interesting about the Sumerian contracts is *where* they were. In the interior, individuals were confident enough about their future to enter into longer-term contracts. At the frontier, nobody had any idea what tomorrow might bring. The future was completely unpredictable, absolutely unknowable. A good harvest might signal bounty, but it also might attract invaders. What were the chances that invaders would show up? Who knew? In response villagers were far less likely to make commitments about their actions in the far-off future.

As we will see, the example provides a telling metaphor for bubble research. While marching Hittites are naturally much less of a concern today, dramatic changes in society and the economy—changes that reshape the economic landscape—occur as a matter of course. Our frontier is conceptual, not geographical, but markets function to this day much differently at the frontier than in the interior. Today new technologies fundamentally change the way we organize our lives. Such changes present us with terribly exasperating challenges, and we often have little to go on. You can tell that you are close to today's frontier when you have no idea what may happen next. You are trying things that no one has tried before.

Why would someone even approach the frontier? For one thing, humans are naturally curious and inventive, and some in particular appear to have an intrinsic need to explore. Perhaps more important, the potential for enormous financial profit depends to a large extent on the presence of uncertainty. Economist Frank Knight raised that point around 1920. He noticed that people who made money did so because they took risks. If everybody agrees that a business will succeed, they all will want to purchase its stock today. The price will be high today, and the potential for enormous gain in the stock price and hence for investor profit will be small. If there is significant disagreement about the future of a business, however, there is a chance that you can buy it for a small sum today and sell it for a lot tomorrow. If the business succeeds, and everybody knows that, the stock will be worth more. Unusually large profits are available only when nobody knows for sure what might happen.

THE REVOLUTION OF UNCERTAINTY

The study of that uncertainty—and the way the human mind responds to it—has started a revolution. There are two types of uncertainty, and the distinction between them is crucial for students of the bubble. The first—which is often called *risk*—is the type of uncertainty introduced because of random factors within the realm of existing human experience, factors that have well-defined probabilities. For financial markets, such risks are discounted all of the time. Frost might destroy an orange crop, for example. Will a frost happen? We have quite a bit of useful statistical information to go on. Significant frosts happen in the major orange-growing region of Florida every few years. We know how much of the orange crop a frost usually destroys, and we can even look at the response of juice prices to the damage. But after the harvest, the risk from frost is gone, and the uncertainty is resolved. People who want to bet on a big increase in juice prices pray for frost. Those who want to bet on low juice prices pray for warm weather. Nature decides the winners. Markets and people function efficiently when faced with such risks. They are easy to think about and easy to quantify, and their resolution is observable.

The other type of uncertainty—which is called *ambiguity*—is the result of the absence of reliable information about future events. If you sail a boat across the North Atlantic for the first time, what are the chances that a sea monster will eat your ship? A scientific genius has walled himself into his garage, intent on finishing a secret invention that he believes will completely alter society. What are the chances that he will succeed?

At the frontier, we are not worried about the weather; rather, we are haunted by ambiguity. There is no reliable information about what might happen, or the probabilities of different eventualities. This ambiguity has a strong psychological effect. Part of us wants to be daring and join the avant-garde with all our energy and resources, while another part wants to stake out a safe and pleasant existence far away from the raging battles. Our markets work to funnel money to the frontier because the potential for profit there is great, but each of us must face that most terrible question: Should I risk my own savings?

Psychological research has taught us a great deal about how we think about such problems. Often we rely on clues and signals—what everyone else is doing, for example—that do not necessarily make logical sense. At that point Adam Smith's model of a rational market begins to strain, and it is there that we may find the primordial froth of bubbles.

How do humans act in the presence of ambiguity? The study of that behavior started with a clever paper published in 1961 by a brilliant young graduate student at Harvard. Daniel Ellsberg had no idea that he was writing a seminal paper on financial bubbles when he asked his undergraduate students to participate in a simple experiment, a game involving two urns. The first contained one hundred little balls, fifty red and fifty black. The second also contained one hundred balls, but students were not told how many were red and how many were black. Students knew that they would win a prize if they selected a red ball and were allowed to pick from either urn. The experiment, since replicated thousands of times, produced shocking results. Students avoided picking from the urn of mystery at all costs.

Ellsberg was an early student of information theory. He performed the experiment because information theorists had concluded that rational students in such a setting should be indifferent between the two urns. Since they had no information about how many balls of each color the urn of mystery held, they should have acted as if the urn contained fifty red balls and fifty black balls. Any combination was possible, and all combinations were equally likely. The logical odds of pulling a red ball were the same for both urns. Yet something bothers us about that conclusion. We can understand it rationally, but our actions often suggest that our intuitive selves are unwilling to act on our logical mind's instructions. Knowing a forecast of a 50 percent chance of rain feels completely different from not knowing the weather report, even in climates with rain every other day.

We have subsequently learned many things from that experiment, and the results have been crucial to bubble researchers. People act differently if a prize is changed to a penalty. Because people in such settings respond to what their friends do, behavior cascades might occur. If your coworker buys shares in a specific company, you might do so, too. The results informed people who study financial markets. Risk, it turns out, is much different from ambiguity, and our behavior can be quite different in situations that might seem quite similar. A person might be fully comfortable wagering $10 on a coin flip, but wholly unwilling to invest in a new business with ambiguous prospects unless his friends are doing it, too.

A TECHNOLOGY FRONTIER

At times there is no place to hide. After the frontier of the Roman Empire fell, the barbarians marched straight through to Rome. In the Internet boom, for example, a basic problem presented itself—a problem that was completely new but rather like other episodes we discuss later in this book. A terrific new technology changed the way that businesses and customers interacted. At the outset nobody knew what to expect, or what probabilities to assign to the different possibilities. Would Pets.com, the upstart Internet pet store, put the brick-and-mortar stores in your neighborhood out of business? It might happen. The e-business had a fabulous marketing campaign with a weirdly charismatic sock puppet ("Look, I am a professional happy puppet thing"). How could any pet owner resist having pet food shipped to the home? Pets.com was a serious threat. If it prospered, all the resources supporting local pet stores across the country might become worthless overnight. Entrepreneurs who believed that they had staked out a healthy, secure livelihood safely nestled in the interior of the old economy would face turmoil. If Pets.com failed, its shares would flutter away to the landfill like moths. By investing in Pets.com, you might become rich overnight. Staying away might mean missing the fast train to prosperity.

During the recent wild swings in the U.S. technology sector, many people used their intuition rather than their reason to make their choices and lost large amounts of money in what many journalists quite loosely called a *bubble*. An area that only daring venture capitalists had explored became heavily peopled with newcomers, and many of them lost substantial sums. The carnage was not as bad as after a barbarian invasion, but the emotional and financial casualties were real. A young San Francisco lawyer was typical. His story was featured in the August 1, 1999, edition of the *New York Times*. The *Times* described a man heavily in debt. How did he get there? Faced with the image of day trading as an easy way to make money, the young man began to trade on his coffee and lunch breaks, between meetings and conference calls. He borrowed "as much as he was allowed against his stock portfolio," and his credit card company lent him $20,000. The lawyer borrowed up to $40,000 to buy securities, primarily in Internet stocks.

The potential payoff was so great that the Californian found it hard not to be sucked into this newfound career. "I was a gambler sitting at a table" in Las Vegas, he said. "My palms got sweaty thinking about how much money I could make." Instead, he lost everything—as did many others. Did these people rush in foolishly? If so, why? What was it about the Internet that led to the frenzy? People have rushed into stocks before and have been called lemmings—yet made lots of money. Did *this* rush cause a bubble?

Many in the media said that it did, but that has nearly always been true when share prices rise. But look at the U.S. stock market over the past half century. The stock market has gone up and up. Every step of the way, some commentators spied a bubble.

There were good reasons to buy stocks in 1999. Given the prior success of Microsoft and the other computer firms, one might even have argued that 1999 was more like 1985 than seventeenth-century Holland. The U.S. stock market entered 1985 on an impressive roll, having skyrocketed over the previous two and a half years. The Dow Jones Industrial Average, a rather boring collection of old-economy stocks, soared from a low of around 700 in the summer of 1982 to almost 1,500. Investing novices were excited and prudent veterans on alert. Was a bubble forming in the U.S. stock market?

The word *bubble* had stayed out of the press for decades, but the surge in stock prices was so striking that

age-old concerns were suddenly renewed. Many saw terri-
fying parallels to early speculative manias. *The Economist,*
the venerable British magazine, was typical of those who
were highly suspicious of the skyrocketing share prices. In
an article published in early May 1985, share prices were
said to be soaring because investors were streaming into
the market "like lemmings." The analogy was clear: Those
foolish enough to put their money in the market at those
high prices would be killed.

But, as is more often the case than not, there was no
bubble. Prices never returned to their previous level. If
you invested in the Dow companies and risked being
labeled a "lemming" by *The Economist* in 1985 (and then
reinvested your dividends), you would have seen your
portfolio increase by almost a factor of ten in the subsequent fifteen years.

Shrill warnings accompany every increase, but sometimes they stick. How can you spot a real bubble? When
does a price increase not signal trouble?

GOOD SWING–BAD SWING

The answers to these questions are within reach. If you are
investing close to a frontier, you need to be especially
wary. Some price movements are sensible, and some are
not. Bubble researchers have divided them into groups and
have found some provocative common themes, which later
chapters of this book develop. What should you look for?

Though not about stock investments, the case of a
Philadelphia man who made one of the largest percentage
profits of all time provides an example of a good price
swing. In the spring of 1989, our collector (who has

remained anonymous) wandered through a Pennsylvania flea market looking for a picture frame to add to his collection. In a far corner of the market, he found a hideous painting, a dark country scene with an illegible signature. The frame, however, was attractive, so he offered the seller $4 for the painting. At home the purchaser separated the frame from the picture and discovered that the frame was crudely made and even less valuable than the painting. He would have to throw the painting and frame away. There was nothing left to save.

Or was there? Behind the back panel was a piece of paper that had been folded to the size of an envelope. When the collector unfolded the paper, he discovered one of only seven unframed and unbacked copies of the Declaration of Independence. Since the painting had protected the copy for so long, it was remarkably well preserved, perhaps the finest remaining copy. When asked to authenticate the paper, Sotheby's experts declared the document as crisp and clear as it was on the evening when John Dunlap printed it. Two years later the copy was auctioned for $2.42 million. Diana Phillips of Sotheby's reported that the seller was "absolutely delighted"—as he should have been. His $4 investment turned into $2.42 million almost overnight.

We can be fairly certain that the purchaser, upon finding that he possessed a rare copy of the Declaration of Independence, suffered no anxiety that his investment would suddenly drop back to its original $4 value. And we can be sure that news stories about his fortunate turn made no reference to mania despite the fact that he made millions overnight. No, the profits were deemed both secure and sensible because the purchaser had discovered something new about the painting after he took it home. The news that the painting contained a priceless American relic justified his enormous profits. That is a "good" price swing.

Such unanimity of opinion does not accompany every happy investment return. At times markets puzzle even the most committed Hayek-believing free-market disciple. Unquestionably, "bad" price swings occur.

One of the most striking examples occurred in the late 1990s. EntreMed was a start-up biotechnology firm with two drugs in early development, Angiostatin and Endostatin. In November 1997, an article in *Nature* implied that the drugs, which stopped angiogenesis (the process by which tumors feed themselves), might be the long-desired cure for cancer.

If such a cure were found, EntreMed would reap enormous revenues. However, history books are full of stories of drug candidates that were promising in the laboratory but disappointing in practice. EntreMed stock rose from $11 to about $15, a healthy increase, but nothing extraordinary.

What happened next *was* extraordinary. On Sunday, May 5, 1998, a front-page *New York Times* article discussed the EntreMed results. To insiders who knew the literature, the *Times* article offered little news. But the article introduced the potential of the EntreMed drug to the general public. It is an understatement to say that people responded with enthusiasm. Everybody wanted a piece of the firm that might find a cure for cancer.

EntreMed's share price was $12 the Friday before the *Times* article. The price opened Monday at $85 per share. The buying frenzy did not stop. The NASDAQ biotech index increased 7.5 percent that day. A few months later bad news was released. On November 12, 1998, the *Wall Street Journal* reported that other labs had failed to reproduce the EntreMed study. The stock fell sharply that day, to $32—still more than twice the price on May 1!

Such swings severely test those who believe that the stock market moves up and down for purely rational reasons. Perhaps the *New York Times* article gave a certain credibility to the earlier *Nature* article, a credibility that might justify a price increase. But should such an event make the prices for all other biotech stocks increase? Why did other firms that were investigating cancer cures see their prices increase? Wouldn't EntreMed's success make their drugs superfluous?

Finding bubbles requires knowing where to look and what to look for. Near the frontier, assets (such as the EntreMed stock) may swing wildly in price for odd reasons that do not relate to fundamentals at first glance. Assets such as the newly discovered Declaration of Independence are akin to the interior of an established country, where there is security and safety. They often increase in value because new information is acquired that signals good news. Examples of both types of movement abound. Later chapters present several simple devices to help the reader identify which circumstance better describes his or her own investments.

In the next chapter, we look back at the work of some of the earliest bubbleologists, and then follow closely the give-and-take that subsequently occurred between countless researchers. After describing the results of their search for bubbles, the final chapter of this book explores the deeper questions alluded to at the outset of this chapter. What does the bubble research imply about the superiority of the free-market system? Will the availability of tools to recognize bubbles lower the chance that they might occur? Since bubble behavior accompanies periods of exploration, are bubbles really a bad thing? Would we be better off if there were no bubbles?

But before we can answer those questions, we must head for the frontier. Such a trip is often perilous without a guide. In 1688, Josef de la Vega wrote the first careful study of unusual market phenomena, *Confusion de Confusiones.* His work took the form of a dialogue about the market between, among others, a person identified as "Shareholder" and a wise "Philosopher." The two gentlemen have kindly agreed to join us in the pages that follow.

CHAPTER TWO

The Price Is Right!

PHILOSOPHER: *Wonderful to see you again, my friend! It's been ages!*

SHAREHOLDER: *Almost four hundred years; thank heavens we are fictional characters! Say—are you still following the market?*

PHILOSOPHER: *Absolutely. And we've really moved ahead since we last met.*

SHAREHOLDER: *That's great, but I am more confused than ever. What bothers me most is the market itself. The press talks about the market as if it's alive—the market thinks, it has mood swings, it turns into different animals. What is the market?*

PHILOSOPHER: *Excellent question. Journalistic discussions of the market can be very confusing. You might try to wean yourself from them. Let me start by asking you a question: Who is the smartest person on earth?*

SHAREHOLDER: *Physics probably attracts the smartest people, and Stephen Hawking is the smartest physicist.*

PHILOSOPHER: *Perfect. Dr. Hawking it is. Now suppose that you were going to engage in a battle of wits with him with a bundle of money at stake. How confident would you be?*

SHAREHOLDER: *Not at all!*

PHILOSOPHER: *Millions of people buy and sell assets. The stock market always picks the price that balances the buyers and the sellers. And at the same time, the market sets the prices so as to balance the good and bad opinions about the stock perfectly. Think about it like this. Stephen Hawking is checking research reports, news stories, personnel files, and so forth. He has all information relevant to determining the price of a stock. Every now and then he punches a new price into his computer. We get to see the results of his efforts, but we do not learn the process or what information was important. We see only the price. That's the best model of the market.*

SHAREHOLDER: *How do we know whether he's doing a good job?*

PHILOSOPHER: *He is Stephen Hawking. Of course he's doing a good job.*

SHAREHOLDER: *But how can I know for sure?*

PHILOSOPHER: *You could make a fortune if you could do a better job. Try it! If you think that the price of General Motors is too low today, then buy it; tomorrow may prove you right.*

SHAREHOLDER: *Well, I'm going to try. I will put all data for the stock market into my computer and search for patterns that suggest that the market is making mistakes. With all those resources I should be able to find some way to make money.*

A chicken farmer does not have to see a fox to know there is one on her farm. Sometimes the only sign of a fox is a missing chicken. The farmer doesn't need to waste time checking whether the farm is fox free if the bed check in the coop holds steady each night.

The search for bubbles began in the early 1960s and relied on a similar observation. Rather than describing the characteristics of bubbles, researchers began by thinking about the behavior of stock market prices if no bubbles existed. They defined *sensible and efficient stock market phenomena* and tested market swings against those standards. If everything looked sensible, they reasoned, they would have no reason to search for the mythical bubble. Before that search even began, scholars were amazingly close to rejecting the possibility of bubbles. Much of this work was summarized wonderfully by Burton Malkiel in his landmark book *A Random Walk Down Wall Street*. The most important lesson of that book—and a necessary prerequisite for the consideration of bubble research—is the observation that the market is extremely formidable, and attempts to outmaneuver it almost always fail. One cannot begin to understand the more recent work that provides exceptions without first pausing to consider the remarkable effectiveness of the market in ordinary circumstances.

What makes a market efficient? The crucial factor is how well the market handles information. In an efficient market all information about a specific stock is immediately built into its market price. Nothing else known today can give a better estimate of the true value of the stock than the market price. An efficient market is like a perfect computer. It wraps up everything relevant into a single price. A well-functioning financial market also rules out bubbles. If madness drives investors to demand more of a stock than is reasonable, the efficient market works to offset those effects. In this chapter we explore in detail how this mechanism works. This background is a necessary first step in our bubble journey. A bubble can exist only if the mechanism fails. One cannot test a mechanism for flaws without first identifying proper function.

Already in the 1920s, Friedrich A. Hayek maintained that the market translates the actions of millions of people into prices with incredible efficiency, as if an omniscient being—or alien Borg collective—could access what each individual knew all at once. Some sort of superpowerful (Hayekian) calculator sets the efficient price.

Hayek argued that free markets are superior to centrally planned economies. Individuals close to the action have much more information about relevant local conditions that govern a decision. The trades between individuals with the best possible information set prices. But a centrally planned government cannot possibly take everything into account from afar.

Economist Thomas W. Hazlett recently described in *Reason* magazine how Hayek's insights related to the origin of the Allied victory on D-day during World War II. He made a strong case that the power of decentralized decision making was a primary determinant of Allied success: "Due to unexpectedly strong tides, landing craft deposited units over 1,000 meters from their prearranged positions. Heavy machine-gun fire pinned down those who managed to reach the beach. Crouching for cover, U.S. infantrymen assembled and spread out their maps. They had no radio contact, and most of their commanders could not be located. The ranking officer quickly made a decision: 'Let's start the war from here.'" The Germans gave no such decision-making power to their troops. Only Hitler had the authority to position valuable military assets such as the powerful Panzer divisions.

Field commanders who wanted to use the tanks to drive the Allies back into the sea were not allowed to act until Hitler approved the deployment. It took hours to gain such approval, and the delay in launching a counterattack was decisive. Quick-thinking Allied officers—who reorganized their troops on the fly after taking heavy casualties—stayed one step ahead of the slow-moving Nazi machine.

How does that wartime experience relate to the stock market? The market would certainly be rational and efficient if all participants in the market were, as well. Each shareholder would pull out a trusty Hayekian calculator, enter all relevant information, and arrive at the perfectly rational price. But the real world hardly looks like that. Undoubtedly some investors buy and sell things for irrational reasons. And some rational and well-informed investors have widely divergent views about the right numbers to enter into their calculators. The first task that economists set for themselves was to understand the possible effect of irrational or misinformed individuals on the functioning of the market. Their first answer was a surprise.

A FOOL AND HIS MONEY

Let's for just a moment assume that there are no fools investing in the market, and let's also assume that there exists a fully rational price for a stock that would hold if only rational and unemotional investors participated in the market. Now let's get back to reality and introduce enough of the imprudent to make things interesting. Suppose that they want to purchase only stocks that are "cool," like Internet search engine provider Yahoo! How do the wild and crazy guys affect prices? Economist Milton Friedman and his colleagues at the University of Chicago argued that foolish investors would have no effect at all. Rational investors, who profit at the expense of fools, celebrate their arrival!

Why? Suppose that many investors buy and sell stocks for irrational reasons. Two possibilities could occur. First, if purchases are completely random, then the effects of the foolish cancel out on average. A foolish bear exists for every foolish bull. But if their actions are somehow coordinated—perhaps they all decide to purchase stocks if the Yankees win the World Series (their victory is a painfully common occurrence)—they might rush in and out of the market at the same time. Then they could influence prices. Even in that circumstance, the efficient-market mavens argued, the imprudent should have no impact on the functioning of the market.

They reasoned that smart money would move in and out of specific stocks if their prices deviated from rationality. If the fools decided that they disliked General Motors for crazy reasons, then the stock would become irrationally cheap. Smart investors could rush in and buy. The smart money would rush toward General Motors stock until the sale ended. In such a fashion the movement of the smart money would offset the actions of those swept up in a frenzy that would otherwise result in mispricings. According to efficient-market theory, the movement would either ensure that the price of each stock remained at its rational price forever or quickly (but not instantaneously) return the price of a stock to its rational level.

A kind of financial Darwinism would also work to promote market efficiency. Over time only rational people would remain in the market. Those who throw their money after shaky schemes can easily be outsmarted. Informed investors will sell overpriced assets to them and watch prices come back to earth. The process can continue until the fools are broke. The sorry fate of the day traders and dot-com fanatics of the late 1990s may provide an example of just that mechanism.

But we are presupposing the existence of a fully rational price. Is it sensible to believe that a price exists for every stock in the universe that all rational beings should agree is the correct price? The first researchers to explore that question answered with a resounding yes. They provided testable predictions about the prices that should emerge in an efficient market. The first evaluation of those predictions supported market efficiency.

Before we look at the evidence, let's consider the remarkable reasoning of the efficient-market theorists. The first key result concerns the fully rational value of any stock at a point in time. Does the market's price make sense? How high can a stock's price go before it becomes irrationally high? Early theorists believed that they had the answer: very high. The second result involves *changes* in the price of the stock, or the ups and downs that a stock takes through time. Do the changes and variations of the market price conform to the predictions of rationality? As we see in chapter 3, if markets are rational (and bubbles impossible), stock price movements take a specific and unlikely form.

COUNT THE CASH

At what price should you be willing to buy a stock? If you were thinking of buying an apartment building, the answer would be fairly simple. First, you could ask a local bank about the monthly mortgage payment. You could check newspapers for comparable rents. After accounting for maintenance and other expenses, you could decide to buy or not. If more cash flows would flow in each month than out, you would be tempted to buy the property.

A myopic inspection of monthly cash flows might lead you to a bad choice. Suppose that rent just covers the monthly cost of a fifteen-year mortgage. Buying the apartment building might be sensible since the mortgage would be paid off in fifteen years, and then the rent would primarily be profit. To make a truly rational decision, you should add up all costs of buying and renting the apartments and the cash flow from rent payments expected over all years that you own the property. You should put less weight on payments in the distant future because those would be worth less today than cash received immediately.

Economists call the task of determining what a dollar delivered in the future should be worth today *putting a present value* on the cash flows. The present-value calculation depends crucially on the interest rate. If you can put money in the bank today and get a fabulous interest payment of 20 percent per year, then $100 will be worth $120 next year. Interest compounds, and that small stake grows tremendously over time. Ten years from now, it will be worth more than $500.

One of the most important results in all of economics is that the value of a firm set by an efficient stock market must equal the present value of the cash generated by the firm. This is a kind of golden rule of finance. Why is it true? The result follows because of *arbitrage,* the riskless buying and selling of assets for a profit. If the price of the firm differs from the present value of all cash ultimately generated by a firm, a simple and highly profitable arbitrage becomes possible. Free money is available to an arbitrageur clever enough to grab it. The mechanism figures prominently in the bubble work discussed in future chapters. If there is a bubble, then it must be because arbitrage failed.

Here's how it works. Suppose that irrational exuberance has driven the price of a firm (Guppies.com) well above the present value of cash flows but not affected the price of some other stock (Very Small Fish Incorporated). Suppose also that in theory the firms are absolutely identical. They each pay a dividend of $5 and should be rationally priced at $50. But the trendy stock sells for $500. As an informed investor who recognizes the mispricing, you can make a quick killing. Here's how. First, offer a person owning Guppies.com the following deal: Let me hold your stock for you, and I will give you whatever cash the stock throws off plus an extra $1. If he ever wants the stock back, you will give it to him. When he gives you the share, you can take the overpriced asset and sell it and use the proceeds to purchase the correctly priced asset. In our simple example, this trade makes you lots of money. You could sell Guppies.com for $500, and then use the money to purchase ten shares of Very Small Fish Incorporated. Those ten shares deliver a combined dividend of $50. Siphon off $6 to pay the Guppies.com shareholder who lent you the stock, and you just made a nifty $44 profit! The example is not fanciful. Many highly profitable hedge funds take advantage of momentary mispricings every day.

This transaction is called *selling short* Guppies.com, and you should replay the game with everyone who will

take the offer—as should any rational investor who noticed the opportunity. This would put downward pressure
on the price of Guppies.com shares. When there are more
sellers of anything, the price goes down.

Free-marketeers have long believed that games like
the one we just played force wacky superstitions out of the
market. If mispricings remained, then profits could still
be realized. Of course this example is highly stylized. For
stocks the real challenge is figuring out whether the price
is right and, if it is not, finding another asset not artifi-
cially inflated by a bubble to set up the arbitrage.

Let's take the next step. What should a stock like
Johnson & Johnson be worth? At what point is the share
price too high? Efficient-market theorists answer that the
correct price can be determined by counting the cash, just
as you would for an apartment building or a bond. If you
buy Johnson & Johnson today, you are purchasing a
stream of dividends that will run as long as the company
operates and is profitable. Put a reasonable value on that
stream, and you have a target price for a rational investor.
If the current market price is well above that, stay away. If
the current market price is well below that, you have
found a bargain.

HOW HIGH CAN IT GO?

Now we can begin our first, crude search for bubbles.
Let's try a real stock and calculate a fully rational value of
the cash stream generated by Johnson & Johnson. We
must make a few assumptions about the future of the company, but we must be careful to consider the possible

effects of changes in assumptions. When we vary those assumptions a bit, we can acquire a feel for the range of rational values. If the actual market price is outside that range, then we have found ourselves a bubble.

At this writing (August 2001), Johnson & Johnson stock is selling at $55 per share and pays an annual dividend of about 75 cents. Only five years earlier the same stock was selling for $10. That increase of more than a factor of five looks suspiciously like the price increase that tulip bulbs experienced in the 1600s. Is $55 too high? Is it a bubble? One simple way to check is to see if expected dividends add up to more than $55. How much cash will a share of Johnson & Johnson deliver?

The amount depends on what happens to that dividend over time. The firm has been able to develop new products, increase its profits, and raise its dividends more than 10 percent per year for many years. Analysts expect the pattern to continue at least for the next five years, with annual growth expected to average about 13 percent. What is that dividend stream worth?

That is an easy spreadsheet problem. If you have never counted the cash, you will be surprised at the value of that humble dividend as it continues to grow over time. Assume that the interest rate to value money in the future is 8.0 percent, about the same as the corporate interest rate. Also assume that Johnson & Johnson will grow its cash flows exactly as the analysts predict for the next five years and then at a rate of 6.2 percent (6.2 percent is the average growth rate for all firms in the U.S. economy since World War II and seems a reasonable assumption). In the first year, the dividend is 75 cents. Next year the dividend will be 85 cents if the analysts are right. Five years from now it will be $1.38 and still growing. What are all of those future dividends worth under those assumptions? Almost exactly the market price as of August 2001—$56.06.

How sensitive is that calculation to changing assumptions? Very! If Johnson & Johnson could grow its dividends at a long-run growth rate of 7.2 percent instead of 6.2 percent, then the present value of its dividend stream would be $121.29, more than twice the current price. If it accomplished only a long-run growth rate of 5.2 percent, then the firm should be worth only $37.40.

Changing the growth rates is a big deal, but the interest rate that we choose has an equally great effect. If we discounted future cash flows with an interest rate of 7.0 percent instead, then the firm's dividends would be worth $127 today. If we chose 6.5 percent to discount future dividends, they would be worth $320 today. If we increased the interest rate to 10 percent, the present value would drop all the way to $26.18.

I chose the first set of assumptions because they seem to be reasonable guesses of what the market might be assuming, but the subsequent assumptions are not unreasonable. The range of prices that could result from the rational function of an efficient market is extreme, ranging in our example from a low of $26 to a high of $320. At what point in that range would we feel comfortable in saying that a bubble has formed and that irrational optimism about future dividends was clearly bolstering prices? The answer has to be, Somewhere near or above the top of that range. Such an answer is not very satisfying because the range is so broad.

What's the practical value of this? Simply that research has demonstrated that counting the cash can support high valuations for most stocks, valuations far in excess of prices in our experience. The approach has even been augmented to allow the analysis of many Internet stocks; "reasonable" valuations far beyond the sky-high values of many firms at the peak of the market have been found as well. Noted economist (and a very likely future Nobel laureate) Robert E. Hall, of Stanford University, drove home that point most forcefully in a historic lecture.

DOT-COMS WITH ANNOYINGLY SENSIBLE PRICES

The American Economic Association invited Hall to give the prestigious Richard T. Ely Lecture at its annual meeting in 2001. The Ely lecture is the most prominent annual economics lecture in the United States; only the most distinguished academic economists need apply. Hall, whose career has been devoted mostly to the study of consumer behavior, chose a surprising topic: the stock market.

The lecture did not disappoint anyone. In a sweeping treatise on valuation and bubbles (referred to in several chapters in this book), Hall carefully explored recent movements in the U.S. stock market and asked the key question on everyone's mind: Had the market gone too high? Were prices out of whack with fundamentals? Using carefully documented statistical arguments, he demonstrated that the data did not support the claim that the entire U.S. market was then experiencing a bubble.

But what Hall did next was shocking. After dispensing with the notion of the market as a whole being in a bubble, he turned to some of the better Internet stocks that had soared so high. He demonstrated that even their prices at their peak were not so high as to be clearly irrational.

Hall had not lost his mind. His calculations were cautious and accurate and highlight an enormously important point: Compound earnings growth is so powerful that very, very high stock prices might be fully rational.

How did he do it? He performed a more sophisticated version of the analysis that we made here for Johnson & Johnson. The valuation problem for dot-coms, Hall wrote, is difficult because their growth today is clearly too high to continue for long. How long does a dot-com take to mature into a firm that stops growing? Nobody knows for sure. But the growth, Hall showed, would not have to continue long for the valuations to make sense.

Hall considered the case of eBay, the online auction business: eBay was expected to post earnings growth of 71 percent between 2000 and 2001. Of course, that could not continue forever. How much eBay should logically be worth depends, however, on how quickly the growth comes back to earth. How fast might the growth decay? Nobody can know for sure, but Hall showed that if that growth declined to zero in seventeen years, then eBay was sensibly priced at its peak at the height of the "bubble." Hall provided the following challenge to those claiming that an Internet bubble existed: "To sustain the claim that eBay, along with the other dot-coms, in early 2000 was obviously overvalued, one would need to show that it was implausible that earnings growth would remain high for more than a decade."

Was such an assumption clearly irrational? Hall said no. Earnings history has so far sided with him, and his analysis even turned out to generate sound investment advice. eBay's earnings growth for 2001 exceeded Hall's assumption—the firm did even better than analysts expected it would at the peak of the "bubble," and the share price has held up nicely.

We return to the Internet in great detail in chapter 8, where we see that the case for an Internet bubble may be stronger than Hall believes, especially for firms that had no cash to count. But his point is important to keep in mind as we explore other attempts to demonstrate that bubbles exist. Often, if you just pull out your Hayekian calculator and count the cash, things don't look as crazy as you might think.

This presents us with a conundrum. Since the calculations of price levels suggest that reasonable assumptions could justify even some of the astonishingly high Internet valuations, we are left with two possible conclusions. Perhaps a bubble never existed, and the price of almost everything has never roamed into an area that requires irrationality as an explanation. Conversely, looking at the *level* of prices might not logically be a powerful test of any theory because small deviations in factors about which we have little information can be so decisive.

The best use of present-value approaches is to employ them to define a kind of comfort zone. An investor should be reassured if the present-value calculations suggest that the current price of an asset is in the low end of the reasonable range and should be concerned if the price is in the high end. This approach is also helpful for identifying bears who have no idea what they are talking about. This provides useful clues about who to ignore. A share price is identifiably too high only if it is outside of a reasonable range that one might glean from the company's cash flows. Absent a prudent analysis of this range, a sell recommendation is nothing more than hot air. But an analyst who makes the case in the proper manner should be taken seriously. In the end, however, it has very rarely been the case that such methods have been able to provide useful sell information, and they certainly have not ever made the case that a bubble exists for all stocks. In the next chapter, we investigate the next logical place to look for signs of a bubble.

CHAPTER THREE

Rational Leaps of Faith

PHILOSOPHER: *Back so soon? Tell me—did you make any money by outsmarting the market?*

SHAREHOLDER: *Sadly, no. My wallet is a lot thinner than it was. Time and again I looked at historical patterns of stock prices and found something promising. But when I tried to take advantage of those patterns, I failed. The market was like a pool shark, drawing me in with the promise of easy victory and then taking me for all I had.*

PHILOSOPHER: *You must have been talking to those journalist friends of yours again! I warned you about that. There are so many different stocks—you can always find a pattern if you stare at history long enough. But few people have ever been able to use those patterns to make money. Have you ever gambled?*

SHAREHOLDER: *Sometimes, but I like my money too much to do it very often.*

PHILOSOPHER: *If you had thought more about our last conversation, your wallet might be a little thicker today.*

Suppose that our model of the market is a sound one, that Dr. Hawking really is sitting in a room and processing all the information about a specific firm. Yesterday he told us that the price of General Motors should be $50. Today he changes that to $55. Why would he do such a thing?

SHAREHOLDER: *Clearly he must have learned something good about the company. Maybe it posted surprisingly good profits.*

PHILOSOPHER: *You used exactly the right word.*

SHAREHOLDER: *Profits?*

PHILOSOPHER: *No, surprisingly. If Dr. Hawking is doing a good job of setting the right price, then he changes the price only if he learns something new that he didn't know yesterday. A price change that occurs when there is no new information is an admission of error. Dr. Hawking changes the price only when something he didn't anticipate occurs.*

SHAREHOLDER: *But he is so smart. How often is he fooled by events?*

PHILOSOPHER: *Not often at all. He is so smart: He predicts events correctly on average, at least most of the time. Sometimes his forecasts of future profits are a little high, sometimes a little low. Over time those errors cancel out.*

SHAREHOLDER: *How can I tell when he'll be wrong?*

PHILOSOPHER: *You can't. He does as good a job as possible predicting the future, and he puts all that information into the price. Indeed, there appear to be two types of firms. The first is those that have a long earnings track record. For these it is easy to decide on a reasonable range, and the market always prices them in that range. The second set is made up of those firms that have little record to extrapolate from. The market prices those, too, but on so little information that its hard to evaluate whether the prices are rational or not.*

SHAREHOLDER: *So I have no chance to do better?*

PHILOSOPHER: *I'm afraid so. I like to think of it this way. The Fates guard the entrance to Dr. Hawking's room. Each morning they wake up and flip a coin. If it's heads, they send good news in to Dr. Hawking, and he raises his prices. If it's tails, they send bad news in, and he lowers them. Try to make money on the day-to-day swings, and you are effectively wagering on coin flips.*

SHAREHOLDER: *I would never wager on coin flips.*

PHILOSOPHER: *You just did!*

What we have seen so far is that the price of a stock can be quite high and still be plausibly related to true fundamentals. Once bubble researchers realized that, they set out to derive alternative tests that would rely on other information. One of their first tasks was to think about the *changes* in prices from day to day and then try to detect bubbles from them. If bubbles are present, such a focus is most promising. It might not be possible to precisely say that Johnson & Johnson should be worth $80 today instead of $50. However, we might be willing to agree that a jump from $50 to $100 in response to news that Tylenol causes cancer would be a decisive sign that craziness is afoot. The search for such irrational patterns is the next logical step.

What should price *changes* look like in a perfect market? Louis Bachelier originated the concept that stocks should follow something called a *random walk.* In his doctoral dissertation at the Sorbonne in 1900, he reasoned that the price today should equal the price that the market expects tomorrow. If the market expected the price of a stock to rise tomorrow, then clever speculators should buy it today; that move would introduce immediate upward pressure. The ups and downs of the price of a stock should be unpredictable and completely random.

Bachelier's highly intuitive notion stimulated an enormous amount of work, beginning in 1953 with the publication of an analysis of British stock and commodity prices by statistician Maurice Kendall, who carefully documented the random-walk pattern in prices. His description of a random walk remains one of the best: "The series looks like a wandering one, almost as if once a week the Demon of chance drew a random number . . . and added it to the current price to determine the next week's price."

By the 1960s the random-walk pattern was fairly well known, but nobody had grasped the connection between random walks and Hayek's calculator. Was a random walk a necessary pattern for prices in an efficient market? Nobody knew. Then, in 1965, Nobel Prize–winning economist Paul Samuelson changed that. He showed that stock prices in an efficient and rational stock market must follow something like a random walk.

An efficient market is one that makes the best possible use of all information available about the prospects of a stock. Samuelson described the best possible use. If the price today equals what the market expects the present value of dividends to be and the price changes tomorrow, something must have surprised the market. Rational expectations about the future will occasionally make mistakes, but they should be correct on average—otherwise they are not rational!

If events proceed according to expectation, the price should not change. The minute the market has information about future prospects of a firm, that information should be factored into the price. Today's price incorporates everything that we know about the future. If we learn nothing new, tomorrow's price should be the same as today's.

With its Hayekian calculator, an efficient market correctly calculates and recalculates the fully rational value of cash flows. If the market changes its expectations of interest rates and growth rates, then the market price of a stock can swing wildly. But the swings themselves should always be in response to news. If yesterday the market thought that Johnson & Johnson should be worth $60 and today the market chooses $100 for the price, *surprising* news about J&J earnings growth or favorable changes in interest rates must justify such a large swing.

The price today is our best guess about the future and should not change tomorrow unless we learn something important about the firm: That concept provides a powerful new test of market efficiency. We might not know exactly what the *level* of the share price should be, but we can recognize a reasonable *change* when we see one.

The random-walk theory also contains a fairly powerful insight about the nature of our world that can be illustrated with a simple example. Suppose that a man starts a walk in Washington, D.C., by flipping a coin. If he flips heads, he takes a step to the northwest. If he flips tails, he takes a step to the southwest. Now add a challenge. You must deliver a message to the man as soon as possible. If he has flipped the coin only a few times, he will be easy to find, very close to where he started. But the farther away he travels, the harder he is to find. If he has flipped the coin a thousand times, your job will be much more difficult. After a million tosses, he could be almost anywhere. The same is true of stock prices. If they follow a random walk, then nobody can say with very much confidence exactly where they will be fifty years from now. Tomorrow, however, they will likely be about where they are today.

The random-walk hypothesis has two other important implications. First, since the market price is the most rational possible price, no trading strategy should ever outperform the market. The random stock picks of a five-year-old child should be expected to perform just as well as the highly touted selections of the highest-paid guru on Wall Street. Second, predicting tomorrow's price change with anything known today should be impossible. Because today's price is based on the best available information, nothing else matters.

CONTRADICTIONS IN THE TWO EFFICIENT-MARKET THEORIES?

The two main properties of an efficient market are strange bedfellows. On the one hand, the market always sets the price equal to the best possible guess of the present value of future earnings. At any moment in time—*any*—that is what the price will be. On the other hand, the path of the price over time is completely random, as haphazard as the flight pattern of a butterfly. Nobody has any idea where it will ultimately end up. Each subsequent movement is governed by the proverbial coin toss. And the fluctuations can be enormous.

Is there a contradiction? Shouldn't a price hold steady if the market is so rational? Actually—no. First, if the market is inefficient and if information slowly affects the price, we might expect a stock's price to move gradually from point A to point B. If the market is efficient, news *immediately* feeds through to the price, so we would expect the price to jump in big leaps as soon as news arrives. Second, since the efficient price is the value today of all future cash flows—and that value is quite sensitive to small changes in parameters—large price swings are to be expected! Every tiny little change in growth rates or interest rates has an enormous impact on the true value of the firm.

The second confusion about the random-walk model involves risk, and it is the question that investors most often raise about the theory. If today's price is the best possible guess of what tomorrow's might be, shouldn't we expect that price to stay the same forever? Doesn't a market that generally increases over time violate the random-walk model? This confusion often arises when analysts do not inform readers that prices follow a perfect random walk only if risk is unimportant. If risk is present, investors require risky assets to get a higher expected return, and the random-walk result no longer holds: Instead, the price of a stock takes a random walk around an upward-drifting trend. But for tiny changes or brief intervals, the risk effect should be imperceptible.

However, the interaction between risk and market efficiency *is* important and presents a stumbling block to identifying bubbles. If a particular strategy gives a higher return than the market index, does that higher return signal market inefficiency or a just reward to investors for higher risk? That question haunts us throughout this book.

VICTORY AFTER VICTORY

With the conceptual link drawn, the search for random-walk-like pattern in price movement took on increased urgency. Eugene F. Fama, an economist at the University of Chicago, demonstrated soon after Samuelson's triumph that stock market price movements are random. To the extent that tomorrow's price deviates from today's, that difference appears to be unpredictable.

Between 1965 and 1978 a flurry of research extended and confirmed these results—always with care to control for the chance that risk might confound the results. The research demonstrated three things.

First, short-run movements in the stock market are almost purely random and unpredictable.

Second, trading strategies that attempt to outperform the market generally do not. For example, mutual funds make less money for their investors than a portfolio of stock selected from a dartboard would. While there have been hundreds of similar studies, recently economist Mark Rubinstein drove home that point in his defense of rational markets. In 1976, as a believer in the efficient-market model, the professor at the University of California, Berkeley, began recommending that the best possible stock market investment vehicle was the Vanguard S&P Index 500 fund. That fund did not try to outsmart the market at all, but rather adopted the strategy of buying and holding the whole market. According to the efficient-market theory, that strategy works as well as one could hope.

Over the entire subsequent period, Vanguard was the sixth best of 120 funds observed. We might observe such a pattern if five firms figured out how to beat the market, but there is an alternative strategy. Since the market is random, lucky and unlucky funds always appear in any year. The key requirement of market efficiency is that last year's lucky funds are not expected to do any better or any worse than the unlucky ones. That is exactly the pattern that is observed. Like a great marathon runner, the market sees its improved results as the race goes on. This has been especially true in recent years. For the last five years covered by Rubinstein's study, the Vanguard fund had the *best* record. He concluded that "we don't even have to justify minimal market rationality by claiming that the better performing funds were lucky because there weren't any!"

Third, the market seems to react sensibly to news events such as earnings announcements. When news hits, the price of a stock adjusts in a reasonable direction by a reasonable amount.

Fama and several coauthors performed the first, and still the best, research in that last area. They set out to understand stock splits. A *stock split* happens when a company announces that everyone who owns one share of its stock will tomorrow own two. At first glance that change should have no impact on the value of a stake in the firm. Before the split, ten shares were worth $100 each, for a total worth of $1,000. After the split, twenty shares worth $50 each would total $1,000.

Why does a company split its stock? Many people believe that companies choose to split so that a lower share price will make the stock easily accessible to low-income investors. Berkshire Hathaway, the conglomerate run so successfully by Warren Buffett, had an explicit policy against stock splits. Because of the success of Buffett's investment, however, the share price skyrocketed (to about $80,000). Berkshire decided to issue a new class of share that was cheap enough so that low-income investors could afford to purchase shares. Another theory about stock splits involves manager anticipation. Managers who expect healthy profit and dividend growth might choose to split in anticipation of coming price increases.

How does the market price respond to splits? Fama and his colleagues found an intriguing pattern. Share prices generally post unusually large increases just before a split but level off immediately after. Prices experience a complete and striking break in the unusual positive price movement at the time of the split.

Those price increases likely reflect the tendency of splits to occur when firms are experiencing unusual prosperity. The market hears the news and expects earnings and dividends to grow sharply after the split. That implication led to the most amazing finding. After a split, firms that failed to increase their dividends saw on average a sharp drop in their share prices. The absence of more good news was bad news! The split ratcheted up expectations; with mediocre growth the price moved accordingly. It's a miracle that such nuances could be seen clearly in stock prices.

SEND IN THE CLONES

Recall that arbitrage is the process that drives bubbles out of the market. Constructing arbitrages is easy if the price of one stock (Guppies.com in our earlier example) gets out of line and if other stocks (Very Small Fish Incorporated) that are essentially identical are themselves immune to the bubble. For the arbitrageur to have the opportunity to make lots of money, each stock must have a clone.

With the amazing diversity of firms traded in the stock market, the existence of a clone for each stock seemed—even in the 1960s—to be the weakest link of the efficient-market theory. And clearly the implication would be the most difficult to test. How can you determine whether some combination of stocks could be a clone of Johnson & Johnson? How can you measure cloneness? Which firm characteristics matter?

While most researchers steered far away from those difficult questions, Myron Scholes—yet another Nobel winner—devised a simple and intuitive test that provided perhaps the strongest evidence of an efficient market. He noticed that every now and then some shareholder would decide to sell a huge block of shares in an individual company. Often such large trades happen for reasons completely unrelated to the prospects of the firm. An heir might sell all the General Motors stock just inherited from a rich uncle. What impact should those trades have? If the market could easily clone each stock, the price of each individual stock should barely respond to those block trades. The background demand for shares of McDonald's stock isn't just a demand for McDonald's, but rather a demand for restaurant and foodstuffs companies that produce cash in a pattern similar to McDonald's. If McDonald's were only a speck in that sea of clones, then lumpy, uninformative trades should be inconsequential, as if one less apple showed up at the marketplace one day. But if each stock existed in its own little universe, the large block trades could lead to massive imbalances between supply and demand. That case would see an enormous effect of the trade on the price of the stock. The *opposite* is true. Large block trades have almost no discernible impact on prices.

AN INTELLECTUAL TOUR DE FORCE

The finding that block trades have virtually no impact on share prices was perhaps the crowning achievement of the efficient-market team. With all the results, the case against the possible existence of bubbles seemed absolutely over-whelming. Price movements looked like unpredictable coin flips. No trading strategies outperforming the market could be found. The market seemed to respond quickly and precisely to news about each firm, with the variation in prices a sequence of rational leaps. And, most important, the mechanism that guaranteed that all of the above should logically be true seemed more reasonable than anyone could have expected. Clones were gobbling up bubbles everywhere!

The true believers in market efficiency, who always advise investors to stay in the market no matter what, are individuals who have been well schooled in these results. And indeed, this evidence is remarkable, and convincing. But this is not where the story ends.

Writing about the unanimity of the vast body of research, Harvard economist Michael Jensen famously wrote, "The efficient markets hypothesis is the best estab-lished fact in all of social sciences." No wonder that a generation of financial advisers schooled at our finest institutions adhere to the efficient-market view. They were trained when it was at its zenith. Few remember, however, that Jensen's comment came in an introduction to a special issue of the *Journal of Financial Economics* devoted to startling new research that cast doubt on the efficient-market hypothesis. A counterrevolution was in the making.

CHAPTER FOUR

Bubbles Everywhere?

SHAREHOLDER: *Your evidence seems sound. But I have a problem with the idea that the market is always rational. Crazy things happen all the time.*

PHILOSOPHER: *Yes. But since the Fates determine the ups and downs, the market is random and almost anything can happen once.*

SHAREHOLDER: *But it's not just once. There was Tulipmania, the Great Crash, the 1987 crash, and the dot-com bubble, to name a few. How much does it take to convince you?*

PHILOSOPHER: *Ahhh, but there have also been countless other times when the price of a stock soared and soared. The media are so interested in saying "I told you so" that they ignore the good news. It's the same tendency that makes a murder page one news and a charity ball a nonevent. The fact that some investments turned sour is not interesting. But it would be interesting if some pattern let you look at ten stocks that just increased in price and determine which went up for good reasons and which didn't.*

SHAREHOLDER: *Has anyone tried to do that?*

PHILOSOPHER: *Of course. And one approach looked most promising at one time.*

SHAREHOLDER: *I knew it! How does it work?*

PHILOSOPHER: *I need two more smart fellows for our little room.*

SHAREHOLDER: *Why not Einstein and Newton?*

PHILOSOPHER: *Perfect. Now suppose that Dr. Hawking, with access to all relevant fundamentals, calculates the exactly perfect price for a stock: $10. He then learns that Einstein is going to relieve him in the room and has developed a new pricing model. Tomorrow, when Einstein arrives, he will set the price at $11. Hawking must set the price at $11 today, even if he has no idea how Einstein's model works!*

SHAREHOLDER: *Why would Einstein do that? Did Hawking make a mistake?*

PHILOSOPHER: *No. Now it gets interesting. Einstein learned that Newton would set the price at $11 when he relieved Einstein. Newton set the price at $11 because he had learned that the person who would relieve him would also choose $11.*

SHAREHOLDER: *Who started the $11 fiction?*

PHILOSOPHER: *Actually, it has to go on forever to exist at all. If at some point in the future a person were to use Hawking's original model, then the whole thing unwinds back to today, and the price stays at $10.*

SHAREHOLDER: *How could such a mistake possibly last forever?*

PHILOSOPHER: *It's not as crazy as it sounds. Suppose that Newton has serious doubts that the price should really be $11 even though he has been told that his successor will set that price. When he shows up at work, he sees that Einstein set the* *price at $11. Einstein's belief that $11 is the right price may influence Newton. Einstein is a smart fellow, after all.*

SHAREHOLDER: *But Einstein set the price at $11 only because he thought that Newton would do the same thing.*

PHILOSOPHER: *Yes, but once Einstein makes the leap, everything changes. His prophecy about Newton's actions is self-fulfilling. Newton sees the $11 price and does exactly what Einstein expects. He doesn't change it. So both of them are right about the price, even though both of them are wrong about fundamentals.*

SHAREHOLDER: *But if I know that they're making a mistake, and the real price is $10, I can surely make money.*

PHILOSOPHER: *Go right ahead. Give it a try!*

Theoretical financial and economic research is most powerful when it demonstrates that a particular result just *has* to be true. If you raise the price of your product, your customers will want to buy less of it. That consequence just has to be true.

After the first wave of researchers showed the logical necessity of efficient markets, and empirical investigation backed efficiency up with hard evidence, an overwhelming intellectual force seemed to be at work in the study of financial markets. For those who believed in stock market bubbles, the jig was up. If markets are efficient, bubbles cannot exist.

In the 1960s, some scholars set out to explore the logical limits of the effects of rationality on stock market prices. As far back as 1936, John Maynard Keynes described the stock market as a beauty contest in which investors need to assess "what average opinion expects average opinion to be," implying that shareholders cared more about the whims of each other than the decimal places of corporate cash flows. Under some circumstances, it was discovered, Keynes was right. The tools of rational investors might not be powerful enough to offset the influence of a herd of maniacs. Efficiency no longer *had* to be true.

The new challenge to the efficient-market theory relied on a level of mathematics and statistics as complex and imponderable as the most advanced theoretical physics. The research began to identify the circumstances in which the presence of irrational investors might undermine the smooth operation of the markets themselves. For the first time, an exact description of a bubble was produced for bubbleologists. At last, they knew what to look for.

THE COMPLEX WORLD

A stock is merely a promise by a company to pay money in the future if it makes healthy profits. Individuals value shares because they need investment vehicles that allow them to put their money away for a while with a positive return. Saving for retirement, college, and a rainy day would be impossible without financial assets to purchase. Firms like to sell individuals their stocks because they can use the money to expand operations and increase profits.

Viewed in that way, the financial market seems simple, not much different from a market for apples. There are suppliers (firms) and demanders (people); under such circumstances there is generally no reason to believe that the market will not do a good job finding a rational price to match their wants and needs.

Or is there? In the early 1980s two men discovered a

crucial distinction that might well make financial markets different. David Cass and Karl Shell of the University of Pennsylvania formulated the new attack on efficient-market theory. In the financial world of the free-marketeers, a rational man could push a stock price to its rational level by constructing clever trades that turned mispricings into profits. If the cash flows of one asset are too cheap relative to another's, then buy the cheap one and sell the expensive one and you make a profit. But what if there are so many foolish individuals that the limited resources available to the rational cannot counteract their influence? And what if the actions of the foolish create weird phenomena that convince even the most rational men to behave in ways that defy conventional behavior? Cass and Shell constructed a clever example in which circumstances could lead fully rational individuals to believe just about anything. Incorrect but self-fulfilling beliefs about the future could cause markets to produce bizarre results. Popular bubble accounts had been referring to exactly that pattern all along.

Here's how it works. Suppose that investors believe that sunspots cause the market to go up and down. Cass and Shell chose sunspots because an economist, William Stanley Jevons, proposed that link in the late nineteenth century and a rather remarkable craze followed. When sunspots are plentiful, the market goes up. When spots are rare, the market drops. If individuals come to believe in such movements, they might happen. Suppose a careful scientific model of the sun suggests that spots will be plentiful next year. Many will want to purchase stocks; their rush to do so will drive up prices. Incredibly, the price movement itself could then reinforce future beliefs about sunspots. A rational man might think, "Last year those sunspot-loving crazies made a fortune. This year I'm going to beat them to the punch." If many investors believe that sunspots help determine prices, others might find it difficult to change the outcome and move the market toward efficient pricing.

When could such self-fulfilling loops emerge? The timing depends crucially on the relationship between financial markets and uncertainty. Consider a simple world where only apples are produced. With ample annual rain, the crop of apples will be plentiful. Without rain, no apples will grow. Access to a reliable weather report makes it easy to figure out how much to pay for an orchard. With a substantial chance of rain, the orchard will be quite valuable. If rain is unlikely, the orchard will correctly be cheap: Who wants trees without apples?

The example is almost identical to the types of formulations relied upon by the free-marketeers. We value the orchard by peering into the future. But our job is easy—there are only two possible conditions: rainy and dry. The uncertainty about the two states is well understood; we even know the chance of rain. But in the real world, as we look to the future, our problem is much harder. How many possible paths can the world take? Clearly an infinite number. In that case all bets are off.

At first, the intellectual and technical challenge of wrestling with infinity discouraged researchers from pursuing the implication. Goaded by the early work on sunspots, researchers have informed us about the logical and reasonable possibilities of financial markets in the real world. What they have discovered is shocking. Efficiency is a necessary property of a financial market only under conditions that are so restrictive as to be nearly irrelevant to the world we live in. Markets function perfectly only if the number of financial assets available to investors is the *same* as the number of possible future states of the world! A world with 100 billion possible future states would have efficient capital markets only if it also possessed 100 billion financial assets, one for each possible state. When fewer assets exist than possible states, sunspots, manias, and fads can become self-fulfilling and self-perpetuating. No rational actor could watch the process and recognize that something odd was happening.

In the real world we observe a much smaller number of financial assets than possible future conditions of the world; it is impossible to hedge against many tangible uncertainties. If extraterrestrials came to earth and taught us how to generate energy for free, everything about our economy would dramatically change. But no active market in assets could promise to deliver shares of General Motors stock for a given price in such circumstances. If such markets existed (and millions of others like them), perhaps we should be willing to accept the logical necessity of efficient financial markets. In their absence we must remain open-minded about the possibility that strange phenomena are common in financial markets.

So bubbles must be possible. The search for bubbles—which seemed unnecessary given the weight and success of efficient-market theory—became more urgent than ever.

WHAT DOES A RATIONAL BUBBLE LOOK LIKE?

The beauty of the new models is their exact description of what a bubble might look like if bubbles truly existed in the wild. A French economist who had taken up residence at MIT was one of the first to set out to describe a bubble precisely and then catch one in the wild. Olivier Blanchard and his colleague Mark Watson showed in 1983 explicitly what form a bubble would likely take.

Suppose that you see that a stock is higher today because of the actions of several foolish investors. You will be willing to purchase the stock even in the presence of the bubble if you can rationally expect the price of the stock to be higher tomorrow. And the price will increase if some other individual is willing to buy it tomorrow. That potential buyer might be willing to buy it only if he knows that someone will purchase the stock from him the day after. Under what circumstance would a sequence of rational individuals support an irrational price? Blanchard and Watson showed that the process must run forever. If humans can *always* expect a new generation of suckers to buy the asset, a market with fully rational investors could produce a bubble.

If such a sequence of events occurred, the share price of a stock would increase over time because at each period individuals would expect it to increase again. The result, which has much of the flavor of the sunspot observations, decouples the link between the fundamental value of the firm and the stock price. Whatever investors believe is possible; nothing necessarily constrains their beliefs to allow fundamentals alone to affect stock prices.

Though mathematically precise, the result is a variant of the greater-fool theory of stock market bubbles. Purchasing the asset at such high prices might be foolish, a rational bubble participant might reason, but if he can count on a greater fool tomorrow buying the asset, he can still make money.

More important, Blanchard and Watson showed that their bubble process could generate boom-and-bust behavior in stock prices and that even such behavior might be consistent with the actions of rational participants. The researchers created a switch that would burst the bubble and send the share price down sharply. The switch would be thrown only if an unlikely random event occurred—if two dice rolled snake eyes, for example. The rational investor would continue to purchase stocks if he expected the return to be high enough (and if he believed that the chances of the bubble suddenly bursting were low enough) that he could still rationally expect to make money in the short run.

If this type of bubble affects prices, it would be easy to observe. The stock market would move up and down far more than one might predict given the ups and downs of earnings and other fundamentals.

ANOTHER LOOK AT THE EVIDENCE

Now that a bubble had been reproduced in the laboratory, the next step was to catch one in the wild. The first set of such efforts aroused intense controversy. They appeared to show that financial markets were enormously inefficient and subject to crazy and inexplicable swings, just as the bubble sages expected!

Robert Shiller at Yale and Stephen LeRoy and Richard Porter of the University of California, Berkeley, performed the work independently and simultaneously. Here is their thought experiment. Suppose that you are watching a sequence of people pass through a doorway.

Your job is to guess the height of each person. If you do well in guessing, you win a prize. If you're wrong, you pay a penalty. And you are given information about the heights of all people who might walk by your room, but the average height of everyone in that group is not your best guess at any time, because tall individuals tend to follow tall individuals just as short individuals tend to follow short individuals.

Under what circumstances might your guesses about the height of the next person be rational? The authors proposed an ingenuous criterion and proved mathematically that it was sensible. If you are trying to make your best guess about the heights, you should be trying to make the least and the smallest errors. You will likely begin with a reasonable guess about the average height of people. As you watch the tall and the short people go by, you adjust your guess—though not sharply. You might start with a guess of 5 feet 10 inches. After watching a number of 7-footers walk by, you might raise that to 6 feet. If 7-footers continue to go by, you might raise your guess even more. If you see a sequence of 5-footers, you might lower your guess.

Shiller proved that a rational sequence of guesses in such a setting should have a simple property. The guesses should move up and down over time far less than the observed heights of the individuals who walk by.

Why all this talk about height? The result has a striking implication for stock market efficiency. The stock market price, according to the discounted-cash-flow model, is a rational *guess* about all future cash flows of the firm. In 1970 the market's estimate of the value of General Motors stock was (if markets were perfectly rational) a sound estimate of the present value of all earnings that General Motors would post from 1970 into the future. We can look back and see how solid that guess in 1970 was because we have a record of how much money General Motors earned for each year. We have only to add up the cash for 1971, 1972, and so on and compare the sum to the 1970 forecast of the sum. We can do the same thing again a year later to see how well the 1971 price forecast cash flows after that. After figuring the fully rational price for several years, we can see if the market moved up and down over time more than that fully rational price did. If it did, the market was not behaving rationally and may have been responding to the kind of madness and euphoria mentioned by bubble believers.

Since the market's price is an estimate of cash flows, it should have much smoother movement than the realized cash flows themselves. The exact opposite was true. The stock market moves up and down over time many times *more* than the fundamental price. It was as if our height guesser would see a seven-footer and then change his estimate of the height of the next person to fifty feet. The volatility of the stock market was far greater than the volatility of fundamentals alone. The result implied to many that the market must have been responding to factors other than fundamentals. Periodically expanding and bursting bubbles must be influencing prices.

Whenever a scientific result challenges the accepted wisdom, tremendous activity follows. The response of financial scholars to that brilliant work was no exception. Every assumption was dissected and stretched to see if reasonable changes in it could reverse Shiller's conclusions. At first the result seemed to hold up well. But in 1986, Nobel laureate and Harvard professor Robert Merton found a crucial problem while working with his colleague T.A. Marsh. Shiller had made an assumption about fundamentals that was flawed. When his work was amended so his assumption was more consistent with reality, his result was reversed.

The assumption concerned *stationarity*. Dividends and earnings move up and down a good deal over time. There is substantial uncertainty about what they will be in the future. Shiller modeled that uncertainty by assuming that dividends were stationary: The dividend could be thought of as being pulled from an urn each period and read out loud to the market—with the same urn being used year after year. If the dividend were unusually high one year, we would expect it to go down in the future.

The assumption of stationarity was common at the time when Shiller wrote up his results because it simplified things. Once you have an idea what the average ball in an urn will be worth, you can make a good guess about the value of balls way off in the future—after all, you will be drawing from the same urn. A rational guess about the value of a draw twenty years from now would be the same as a rational guess about the value of a ball one thousand years from now.

But Marsh and Merton noted that the fundamentals for stocks do not look stationary at all. Dividends and earnings tend to grow. If you want a reasonable model of that growth, you need to change the conceptual experiment completely. We should think of earnings and dividends as being drawn from a new urn each year. The balls in a new urn have on average a higher value, and investors will expect dividends and earnings to grow, not stay the same. The change makes all the difference in the world. A surprise in fundamentals should change a rational assessment of how much dividends will *grow* and what the average value of the balls in all future urns will be. Put that property into Shiller's model, and excess volatility no longer implies market irrationality. Humongous price responses to news about fundamentals can be quite rational.

A simple real-world example illustrates how it works. Suppose that you owned Procter & Gamble stock in the mid-1980s. In 1985 and 1986, P&G paid a dividend of 33 cents per share. In 1987 and 1988, it paid a dividend of 34 cents. In 1989, the dividend jumped to 38 cents. If Shiller's model were correct, investors would look at that jump and think to themselves, "We sure were lucky today, but the dividend should go back to 33 or 34 cents, so let's not get too excited." According to Marsh and Merton, investors should have thought, "The growth rate of dividends has just gone up. If Procter & Gamble can continue that, dividends will be a lot higher and share prices should be a lot higher, too." As it turned out, that view was correct. By 2001 the P&G dividend had climbed all the way to $1.40 for the same share of stock. Those higher dividends had an enormous impact on the price of P&G, which quadrupled in value over the same time.

A flurry of recent research has adjusted prior tests to account for those considerations and has produced a mixed bag of conclusions. Some research has corroborated evidence that a share price may move too much even if one accounts fully for those new factors. Even so, other research intimates that the patterns do not suggest that the excess volatility results from bubbles. As work continues, the current state of affairs is this: A result that at first seemed a silver bullet to the heart of the efficient-market hypothesis now appears to suggest that something strange may be happening, but we cannot be sure.

Many bubble-crying pundits, however, refer to this

work when claiming that markets don't work. *New York Times* columnist Paul Krugman, for example, stated in a recent column that share prices obviously fluctuate more than could be explained by the functioning of a rational market. There may have been a point in the early 1980s when the available evidence pointed in that direction. The evidence available today, however, does not sharply contradict efficient-market theory.

EXPLODING PRICES

A stock price might contain a rational bubble if investors today believe that they can sell a stock to someone else at a higher price tomorrow, and so on. One strategy was to search for such a bubble by comparing the ups and downs of share prices to those of the fundamentals. But their work suggests that a different search strategy may be even more effective. If a bubble exists, the share price will move up and *up* over time for no reason. We might observe, for example, the price of General Motors climb from $25 per share to $50 per share over a number of years at the same time that its earnings and dividends remain constant.

In the late 1980s, several researchers showed that the sharp uptrend in dividends—which proved such a nuisance to volatility tests—actually allowed an alternative test for bubbles. If a bubble is not present, the trends over time in the share prices of firms and in the fundamental variables should be almost identical. If dividends go up and up, the share price should, too. If dividends go down, the share price should follow. When a bubble is present, the linkage fails: The price might wander one way while the dividend wanders another.

A pioneering study in the area was published in 1988. Behzad Diba and Herschel Grossman documented a close linkage between the trends of stock prices and their fundamentals. Using stock price and dividend data from the U.S. market between 1871 and 1986, they found a surprising alignment. Share prices soared because dividends did. When share prices tanked, they were following dividends down. After accounting for the trends in fundamentals, Diba and Grossman could find no evidence of a bubble in stock prices.

Perhaps they were using a weak test? As a check of their method, they used their computer to generate artificial data that by construction had a bubble in it. For those data, the common trend technique easily detected a bubble.

There is little evidence that the long-run trends in stock prices are inconsistent with the movements of fundamentals. If bubbles existed in the U.S. stock market, they must have been of the bursting-bubble variety, periodically inflating and deflating share prices but ultimately canceling each other out. If those bubbles burst quickly enough, trend analysis would miss them.

NO SMOKING GUNS

The first wave of researchers who applied scientific methods to the search for bubbles in share price data for the market as a whole found little evidence consistent with bubbles. It is one thing to cry "bubble." It is another thing altogether to define one and see if the predicted bubble properties are observed in actual prices. While theoreticians established the logical possibility of bubbles, attempts to isolate them in the wild were generally unsuccessful—possibly because markets are indeed rational and bubbles do not exist anywhere, or possibly because some firms experience them and some don't. In the latter case, inspection of movements of the market as a whole may not be a powerful method. Bubbles could lurk beneath the surface. In the next chapter, we explore that possibility.

CHAPTER FIVE

The Farmboy and the Fugitive

SHAREHOLDER: *I didn't make any money—again. I couldn't find one stock that Dr. Hawking had mispriced.*

PHILOSOPHER: *What did you find?*

SHAREHOLDER: *At times I thought I saw promising patterns in the prices of the second type of firm we were talking about. Those businesses set out to do something new. But there wasn't any historical evidence to process—my computer model was no help. Dr. Hawking set a price for each one anyway. I have no idea if his prices made any sense, but I was unable to make money by betting against him.*

PHILOSOPHER: *If bubbles affected what we understood most, then they would be easy to detect, and they would have been identified long ago. You have made a lot of progress—I suppose I should share something with you. For some time I have been working on a machine that can detect bubbles, a bubblescope. Let me show it to you.*

[They walk through a door into a room so tall and wide that the ceiling and walls cannot be seen. A large rubber ball is

expanding slowly. In one corner is a telescope. A mechanical calendar stands next to the telescope.]

PHILOSOPHER: *I invented this device to help me search for bubbles. It has two parts. The ball in the center of the room represents the economic universe. The ball gets larger and larger as our knowledge expands. The outer edge of the ball represents the economic frontier. At each point in history, the newest and most revolutionary events are etched on the outer edge of the ball. As the ball inflates, what was at the frontier of our understanding moves to the interior. Let me show you. [He turns the mechanical calendar to the date 1637, and the ball deflates sharply.] I have just set the date to the peak of Tulipmania. What do you see?*

SHAREHOLDER: *(peering through the telescope): All sorts of data and news stories about tulips are etched on the outer surface. Tulips just arrived from Turkey. Nobody has them in their gardens yet, but everyone wants them.*

PHILOSOPHER: *How much money could a tulip producer make?*

SHAREHOLDER: *Consumer demand suggests that the business will be promising, but there is not enough to go on. Who could possibly know? But look at those bulb prices!*

PHILOSOPHER: *Now let's run the calendar forward a bit. [He turns a knob to 1920, and the ball inflates to four times the size.] Now what do you see?*

SHAREHOLDER: *(still using the telescope): The outer edge has some stories about Thomas Edison. He seems to have harnessed electricity in a way that will have many applications.*

PHILOSOPHER: *What about the tulips?*

SHAREHOLDER: *The tulips have been around for centuries. All the information about tulips is in the center of the ball.*

PHILOSOPHER: *Could you have priced a tulip stock in 1920?*

SHAREHOLDER: *Of course. By then there was lots of historical information to go by.*

PHILOSOPHER: *What about General Electric?*

SHAREHOLDER: *It's in the same state that the tulips were back in the 1600s.*

PHILOSOPHER: *Exactly. And your computer model would have some trouble pricing the stock back then, wouldn't it? Now you've learned the most important thing: where to look for bubbles.*

As the second wave of research began to cast doubt on the efficient-market theory and open up the possibility that bubbles existed, research took another direction—one with surprisingly powerful implications for bubble research. An incandescent young man from rural Illinois had started that inquiry almost fifty years earlier, but his work had little tangible effect on research for forty years. After an earth-shattering experiment—proposed by a man who became one of the twentieth century's most famous fugitives—all that changed.

THE FARMBOY FROM ILLINOIS

Frank Knight was not an obvious candidate for international academic fame. He grew up on a farm in Illinois. Leaving high school before graduation, Knight attended two small, not-well-known colleges. But his 1916 doctoral dissertation at Cornell University is one of the great intellectual achievements of the past century. Published in 1921, *Risk, Uncertainty, and Profit* was the first attempt to demonstrate systematically the practical importance of uncertainty to businesses and individuals.

Knight emphasized the crucial distinction between risk and what he called *uncertainty* but which is often called *ambiguity* or *ignorance.* If you are betting on a coin toss, you are taking a known risk. If you bet on heads, you will win 50 percent of the time. Uncertainty presents you with a different problem. A situation is uncertain, according to Knight, if you have absolutely no idea of the probability of each possible outcome. You are forced to make a decision in a state of partial or complete ignorance.

Knight considered repetition the key concept. If we have a lot of experience with a particular activity, we can form beliefs about potential future events that are sensibly based on that experience. If you've seen a hundred throws from a particular pair of dice and the numbers appeared purely random, you might have logically concluded that the dice were fair. But if an acquaintance wanted to engage you in high-stakes craps—with his dice—then you might wonder.

Knight argued that the different forms of uncertainty create dramatically distinct circumstances. Your betting behavior in craps with dice that you know are fair will differ from your behavior when you just don't know. In the real world, Knight added, we usually find ourselves in circumstances where ambiguity and ignorance dominate.

While the observation might seem obvious, it contradicted the type of reasoning relied upon by the free-marketeers. Most students of the markets thought that random chance provided the biggest planning challenge for businesses and individuals. Knight disagreed. He sounded a clear warning: If you ignore the difference between ambiguity and risk, you cannot understand the markets. If we have lengthy and informative experience with a particular business activity, other people probably do, too. According to Knight, we can't realize great profits from businesses that we fully understand. There's too much competition. If we really want to make money in business, we need to fill an empty niche.

If Knight is correct, the kind of decisions most important to a business, and most important to the value of stocks, are made in a circumstance of extreme ignorance. Firms and investors cannot carefully and rationally assess the probability of each outcome. Behavior in such a circumstance is far from behavior in the face of known risks. Without knowing the exact probabilities, firms need to develop other, more heuristic decision mechanisms. Pure reason is not enough without all the facts. Sometimes you have to fly by the seat of your pants.

Knight's work anticipated by nearly fifty years the frequent intellectual conflicts of two great men: James T. Kirk and Mr. Spock. Kirk, captain of the starship *Enterprise* on the television and film series *Star Trek,* flew by the seat of his pants and argued that life was more like poker than chess. Spock, an unemotional alien from the planet Vulcan, prided himself on his mastery of pure reason. To Spock, all uncertainty was what Knight would call *risk.* Each time the *Enterprise* entered a perilous situation, Spock would recite to Kirk the exact probability of the *Enterprise*'s survival. The probability was almost always absurdly low. Kirk recognized that the true chances of survival depended on factors that defied simple probabilistic characterizations, including his own actions. The true probability of their survival was likely unknowable. In such circumstances Kirk used his instincts, much to the dismay of the superrational Spock.

Knight argued that economists had spent too much time developing an understanding of Spocklike rational beings, which made their insights practically useless. If we want to form conclusions about what is possible in our world, we need to understand Kirk. Even Spock might have to agree. The *Enterprise*'s survival suggests that his superrational probabilities were incorrect. Perhaps Spock left something out of his calculations.

VULCAN PERFECTION

John Maynard Keynes seconded and expanded Knight's work in his famed *Treatise on Probability,* which emphasized the practical importance of imperfect human judgment in the study of economic behavior. Hayek also recognized Knight's importance. In 1945 he wrote that research that "starts from the assumption that people's knowledge corresponds with the objective facts of the situation, systematically leaves out what is our main task to explain."

Afterward Knight's ideas fell into relative obscurity, probably for two reasons. First, researchers tend to focus on problems with a hope of a solution. If we allow chance to enter our decision process with known probabilities, we have a mathematical problem that is at least manageable. The mathematics of probabilities had been studied extensively for centuries; economists can draw on that work when formulating theories about behavior under uncertainty. Knight's uncertainty, while intuitively plausible, was something else again. Ambiguity is easy to recognize in practice but difficult to define precisely.

Second, the efficient-market paradigm that evolved

in the 1950s appeared to rule out the possibility that Knightian uncertainty would have much of an effect on anything. A fellow from Detroit with a country music star's name, Jimmie Savage, was the most important player at this point. After receiving his Ph.D. from the University of Michigan, he studied applied math at the Institute for Advanced Study in Princeton, where he was a valued colleague of Albert Einstein. His classic *Foundations of Statistics* is still studied extensively, but Savage's most important contribution from his exploration of behavior and uncertainty is his work on subjective probabilities.

Savage set the following problem: How does rationality limit behavior under uncertain circumstances? Well aware of Knight's work, Savage explored the limits of rationality on individuals without a perfect knowledge of the probabilities of future events.

He listed "axioms" that should apply to a coherent and rational decision. If I prefer apples to oranges and oranges to bananas, I had better prefer apples to bananas. In an astonishing intellectual accomplishment, Savage demonstrated that rational behavior under uncertainty requires individuals to use their best guesses about the probabilities of future events—their own subjective probabilities. If individuals are rational but have their own beliefs about the future, they will nonetheless act as if they were the perfectly rational Vulcan agents.

If Savage's conclusion is true, the efficient-market theorists have almost made a decisive case for their view. While individuals might disagree about the probabilities of future events, they all react rationally and consistently, given their own beliefs. Those with the best information might be able to trade with others who have less information and make money. That process itself will make the markets efficient.

ELLSBERG'S PARADOX

That view was challenged by the work of a man whom Nobel Prize–winning economist Wassily Leontiev described as one of his brightest students. Raised in Highland Park, Michigan, Daniel Ellsberg spent most of his youth virtually chained to a piano; his mother was convinced that he would become a famous pianist. Turning his attention to his academic work, he graduated third in his Harvard class. His graduate career at Harvard, after a sojourn in the U.S. Marines in the mid-1950s, was even more impressive. Ellsberg's doctoral dissertation in economics, published in 1961, set off heated debates. But his ultimate career choices took him far afield from bubbles.

After graduate school, Ellsberg joined RAND, the renowned think tank, and began working on defense policy. Motivated by extreme patriotism, he volunteered for the U.S. forces in Vietnam, where he distinguished himself with almost reckless bravery. The Pentagon commissioned Ellsberg to write a comprehensive history of the Vietnam War. But what he found shocked him and transformed his attitude. Ellsberg decided that the government, from the president down, had systematically misrepresented the conflict to the American people: The war was a lost cause, and the government had behaved dishonorably.

Ellsberg leaked three thousand pages of history to the *New York Times,* which began publishing them on June 13, 1971. The government quickly declared him a fugitive.

Ellsberg vaulted to international fame and spent the next three decades as an antiwar activist. His contributions are clearly of historic importance, but their cost is high. We might be much further along in the study of bubbles if he had continued his economic studies.

Ellsberg's 1961 paper moved Knight's distinction between risk and ambiguity to the academic center court. Savage had convinced most scholars that individuals acted rationally on their own beliefs about the probabilities of different events. Ellsberg demonstrated that Savage had left out an important factor—and he started an entire field that is producing the most intriguing research on bubbles.

Ellsberg's thought experiment, already sketched in chapter 1, is deceptively simple. Suppose that an urn holds one hundred balls: fifty are red and fifty are black. If you predict the color of the ball that you pull out of the urn, you get $10. What color will you choose? Classical probability theory says a lot about the right answer. Since the chance of pulling out either color ball is fifty-fifty, you should be indifferent to the two choices. When forced to choose, participants pick red and black equally.

Traditional probability theory does a good job describing behavior in a second experiment. A new urn, the urn of mystery, holds one hundred balls. Some are red and some are black—but the exact number of each color is unknown. If you can correctly predict the ball's color before you pull the ball from the urn, you get $10. Which color will you choose? Theory suggests that you are indifferent. Since you have absolutely no information about the distribution of the two colors, you act as if there is an equal chance of pulling out either color. That indifference implicitly defines the probability that you assign to each color. If there were fifty-one red and forty-nine black balls, you would clearly maximize your chance of winning if you bet on red. Only a fifty-fifty split is consistent with indifference. Experiments confirm that individuals act rationally in the game, with about half betting on each color.

Ellsberg's historic experiment amended the game subtly but decisively. In a third game we bring in two urns. The first has one hundred balls, fifty red and fifty black. The second, the urn of mystery, has one hundred balls, but the proportion of the balls is unknown. You are asked to pick a red ball from the urn of your choice. Which urn will you use? Ellsberg noticed that most people prefer to pluck a ball from the urn with fifty red and fifty black balls. Participants avoid the extra ambiguity of the second urn.

The avoidance of the urn of mystery is a logical contradiction: By choosing the urn with known probabilities, you act as if the urn of mystery holds fewer than fifty red balls. When you are indifferent to the red and black balls, you reveal an implicit belief that there are exactly fifty red balls in the urn of mystery. Both beliefs cannot simultaneously be true!

Although Ellsberg did not conduct formal laboratory experiments, he recruited some economic luminaries to test his premise. Several, including Savage himself, behaved illogically and inconsistently with Savage's version of pure probabilistic rationality. Why should that behavior matter? The choice of the first urn, with a wariness of the second, conflicts directly with the theory of rational choice, the foundation of the efficient-market view. If even the super-rational designers of the efficient-market theory act strangely when confronted by Knightian uncertainty, can we expect financial markets to be fully rational?

Even after being informed of the apparent irrationality of the choice described by Ellsberg, respondents continued to avoid the urn of mystery. This was even true of many of the economists that Ellsberg asked to participate in his experiment, although he did not ask Savage to play the game twice, writing that he was "reluctant to try him again."

This explains the enormous impact of Ellsberg's work. The stubbornness of individuals to stick by their choices suggests that the experiment identified an indelible behavioral pattern. Normally people change their behavior after an "error" is pointed out to them. With ambiguity, however, individuals stick to their guns. They know that they don't like ambiguity, and they avoid it when possible. Ellsberg's experiment demonstrated for the first time what noneconomists knew all along: People are more like Kirk than Spock. They surf through a world that does not always present problems with explicit and logical solutions.

The observation is vital to bubble theory because a world with no bubbles is a world of Spocks. And in a world of Kirks, anything may be possible.

WHY DO THEY DO IT?

While Ellsberg identified thought-provoking behavior, was it important for financial markets? Are such ambiguous circumstances common?

To Nobel Prize–winning physicist Murray Gell-Mann, ubiquitous ambiguity is perhaps the crucial salient aspect of human existence: "People are scared by the unpredictability and especially the uncontrollability of much that we see around us . . . [Much of this] comes from the restricted range and capacity of our senses and instruments: we can pick up only a minuscule amount of the information about the universe that is available in principle. Finally, we are handicapped by our inadequate understanding and by our limited ability to calculate."

The case for the importance of ignorance is quite sound. Introspection suggests that people face two kinds of uncertainty that efficient-market theorists assume away. The first is uncertainty about what might happen, what states of the world might be experienced. No one can be aware of and account for all possible future states of the world. Second, even for the limited states that we can conceive of, we do not know with certainty the probabilities associated with each. Is there enough uncertainty to affect financial markets?

The question is relevant when we have limited evidence but must evaluate something. Think of the problem of rating a baseball team. Each team has a potentially knowable probability of winning. If a team wins 70 percent of its games, it has a strong chance of making the playoffs. If a team wins 50 percent, it will not. Suppose your team has won seven games—ten games into the season. At that time the best estimate of their underlying strength—based on probabilities only—is that it will win 70 percent of the games. Should you make reservations for the playoffs? Probably not. If your team has won seventy of one hundred, you might make plans (unless your favorite team is the Boston Red Sox, whose potential for doom has achieved such improbable heights that the team has become a challenge to modern science).

Ambiguity and ignorance challenge our minds. If

humans had been purely logical beings, calculating along with Mr. Spock the precise probability of each possible event before acting, then we might have ended up in the dustbin of genetic history. From the dawn of time, circumstances required our ancestors to make decisions based on an incomplete picture of the world. Suppose that a few primitive men are sleeping in the forest. They hear a twig break. Is a tiger approaching? A squirrel? What principles should they use to choose their optimal actions? With all the advances of modern science, we might be able to turn on our supercomputer and derive a sound recommendation for the primitive fellows. Without such access, our ancestors miraculously did just fine. They relied on intuitive skills, honed by evolution, to formulate strategies in ambiguous situations.

Perhaps our strong intuitions concerning the Ellsberg paradox and our unwillingness to yield when presented with evidence that our choices are irrational reflect our reliance on skills that have developed over millennia to deal with complex and ambiguous situations—skills that have served us well. Our gut may do a better job in such situations than our heads.

WHAT DO WE DO?

Ellsberg's view of the world may be more accurate than Savage's; the rationality of our choices may be defensible on evolutionary grounds. Graduating from the simple urn experiments, researchers had to construct a detailed, realistic portrait of human behavior in ambiguous circumstances. The work proceeded in two steps. First, researchers had to confirm and extend Ellsberg's experiment to broader contexts. Second, they moved from the rather technical study of ambiguity alone to discover behavioral regularities with important financial market implications. For bubble researchers the research has suggested four important conclusions, often supported by numerous studies. For the sake of brevity I cite only the most representative.

Many people are highly averse to ambiguity. The first formal confirmation of Ellsberg's paradox in psychological experiments came in 1964. Selwyn Becker and Fred Brownson presented subjects with an ambiguous circumstance and observed their decisions. About half the subjects responded in a paradoxical way: They were willing to pay real money to avoid ambiguous circumstances. Ken MacCrimmon suggested the real-world importance of the result in 1968. His study involved businessmen. About half were wary of beginning an enterprise in a country where a similar business had never existed. In 1995, economists Robin Hogarth and Howard Kunreuther devised an ingeniuous demonstration of the importance of ambiguity. They studied a decision that we have all faced often: whether to purchase an extended warranty for a new electronic device.

When you purchase a computer, a salesperson often offers an expensive extended warranty. To make a rational decision, you need to know the probability that the computer will break and the size of the typical repair bill if it does. We seldom have that information at our disposal. If you ask the salesperson how often the machines break, you get no answer. Kunreuther and Hogarth hypothesized that electronics stores have chosen not to make the strong probabilistic case for an extended warranty because they sell more when ambiguity-averse consumers are completely in the dark. They constructed a clever experiment that documented the case.

People can't be convinced to give up their aversion to ambiguity. Several studies have attempted to persuade subjects to behave otherwise. In 1974, Paul Slovic and Amos Tversky found that students who were informed about the logical contradictions implied by their choices in the Ellsberg game stuck with them anyway. This result has been repeated many times.

People who are averse to ambiguity are not necessarily averse to risk. Experiments that attempt to determine which participants are especially risk averse and which are especially ambiguity averse find that they are often different people. One person might love to gamble but shy away from ambiguity. The dichotomy reinforces Knight's view that risk and ambiguity are distinct phenomena.

People care what others think. In ambiguous circumstances it is easy to sway the decisions of psychological subjects. If you see a person choose the urn of mystery, you become more willing to choose it. The pioneering work in this area was performed by Solomon Asch in the 1950s. Asch performed experiments where subjects were asked to answer simple questions such as "Which line is longer?" after observing others answer the same questions. If other subjects answered the questions incorrectly, then the subjects tended to follow suit. A recent review of 133 follow-up studies concluded that there is very strong evidence of a "conformity effect" whereby individuals place a great deal of weight on the opinions of others, especially if those opinions seem unanimous.

These conclusions are consistent with Ellsberg's proposal. Individuals systematically behave in apparently irrational ways, at least in the sense of the rationality necessary for the efficient-market models. The broad and repeated confirmation of those phenomena in experimental settings strongly influenced efficient-market theoreticians. What impact could all these phenomena have on the movement of prices in financial markets? Does the tendency of individuals to reinforce each other's beliefs in ambiguous circumstances lead to bubbles?

LINKING AMBIGUITY AND FINANCE

The concept of Knightian uncertainty was a powerfully destructive intellectual force. It showed up the analysis of an entire generation of researchers as incomplete and inadequate and raised serious questions about their conclusions, which most students of financial markets had accepted with almost religious fervor. The importance of the perception of ambiguity became widely accepted. But the research had no practical application unless someone could contrive a way to study and model firms and people formally in an ambiguous world so that predictions could be made and tested and new theories could be confirmed or rejected. What does the market look like? Until the 1980s, nobody had any idea.

Centuries of mathematical study of the theory of probability by such giants as Pierre Fermat and Blaise Pascal set a firm foundation on which the free-marketeers constructed their efficient-market theories. Ellsberg's paradox suggested that the work had to be redone on the right foundation. But no new foundation existed. The predicament changed dramatically when highly motivated scholars began to discover alternative ways to incorporate ambiguity into their models of the world. Most important, the new scientific theories led to surprising and testable implications.

ON THE PATH TO KNOWLEDGE

Knightian uncertainty confronts us when we have to make a decision without complete information. If you are running a business and facing ambiguity, you still try to make the most money possible. But how do you do that? Before Ellsberg, economists thought that they had a good idea. By the 1980s that was true no longer.

David Schmeidler, an Israeli theoretician, came up with one of the first alternative approaches. He and Itzhak Gilboa proposed a world with two types of people: those who liked ambiguity (optimists) and those who feared ambiguity (pessimists). Thinking back to the urn of mystery, a pessimist might think, "My best guess about the probability that I pull a red ball from the urn of mystery is 0.5. But since the situation is ambiguous, I'm going to act as if the chance is really lower than that." An optimist might tell herself, "I don't really know the probability in the urn of mystery. It could be much higher than 0.5. I like my chances!"

The researchers then put the two types together and asked, What types of decision rules will these people use when ambiguity is present? Their results were intuitively appealing. When there is ambiguity, a pessimist tends to assume that the worst might happen and tries to choose actions that make the best of the circumstances. The strategy is called the *maximin strategy*. Think back to our twig-snapping example. If you hear a twig snap, a tiger or a squirrel could be lurking. When deciding what to do, your best choice is to assume a tiger and act accordingly (grab your spear). An optimist tends to assume that the best will happen and tries to act so that he receives the highest possible reward. The strategy is the *maximax strategy*. Such a person would go back to sleep and assume that a possum stepped on the twig. (This specific example may explain why humans are naturally averse to ambiguity. Those who were not were eaten.)

To test the model, we need to move from the fictional world to the real world. A simple illustration highlights what researchers have looked for. A farmer has to decide what crop to plant. He can choose between wheat and watermelons. He does not know what the weather will be. If rain comes, all of his crops will grow well. Without rain, only the wheat will thrive. Let's consider the three types of possible uncertainty. If the farmer knows the chances of rain, he will plant both wheat and watermelons—but a high proportion of watermelons if the chances of rain are good. If our farmer has no information about the rain, he is living in Schmeidler's world. If he is averse to ambiguity (a pessimist), he will assume a little rain and plant only wheat. If he loves ambiguity, he will assume lots of rain and plant only watermelons! The predictions are complete opposites.

There are a number of applications to finance. Suppose that two types of traders are in the stock market, optimists and pessimists, and that significant ambiguity exists. Optimists and pessimists will have different trading ranges for a given stock. A pessimist will look at the ambiguous world and think, "If the price is $10, I know that a stock is a good deal, and I will buy it. If the price is $15, the price has gone too far, so I will sell. If the price is in between, I will hold off since I am not sure whether it is too high or too low." The optimist will think that the ambiguous world will smile on him. He will say, "If the price is below $17, the stock is cheap, and I am buying, but if it gets above $25, it has gone too high, and I'll sell." Suppose that the market price is $18. The pessimist will think that the price has gone too high and will sell to the optimist. If the price is $14, the optimist will want to buy, but the pessimist will not sell!

Such models can describe several unusual real-world phenomena, from the behavior of dealers who set the gap between buying and selling prices on the floor of the stock market to patterns of excessive price movement. Scholars have provided insight into one of the more puzzling mysteries of the markets, the tendency of markets to stop functioning occasionally for a short time. When a wholly unexpected and important event happens (perhaps a declaration of war), ambiguity increases dramatically. Optimists and pessimists become more unsure of what the right price will be, and the uncertainty leads to higher ranges where no trading occurs. If Knightian uncertainty is important after major shocks, all activity might even come to a halt. Exactly that has happened—most recently after the terrorist attacks of September 11, 2001—when consumers and firms adopted maximin wait-and-see postures.

Other researchers have studied the impact of Knightian uncertainty on portfolio choice. Individuals might think that less ambiguity surrounds companies that they have experiences with. There is substantial evidence that those beliefs affect purchases. People tend to buy stocks disproportionately from their own country. Strong evidence points to a disposition to buy stocks in certain regions of a country. Investors tend to purchase the stock of telephone companies that operate in their home regions, for instance.

WHERE IT ALL FITS IN

Knightian uncertainty exists when decision makers do not have all the information needed to think rationally about a problem. Over the past four decades, researchers have verified that such uncertainty has a strong and systematic impact on human behavior. They have constructed models that account for ambiguity and have derived testable implications from them. Empirical researchers have confirmed the presence of the predicted phenomena in real financial markets. All pieces of the puzzle are fitting together.

Recall from chapter 4 that Cass and Shell proved that bizarre sunspot phenomena are theoretically possible if the possible conditions of the world outnumber the financial assets available to investors—that is, if markets are incomplete. When would the markets be so limited? Exactly when we find Knightian uncertainty! If we do not know *all* of the things that might happen, then we can certainly not provide an asset for each possible event. With only incomplete information about the future, there is significant ambiguity. The reverse is also true. Since researchers have demonstrated that ambiguity is present, we can say that real-world markets are almost certainly incomplete. The work discussed in this chapter proved beyond a shadow of a doubt that Knightian uncertainty strongly affects behavior and the financial markets. Weird bubble phenomena must be possible. But is there hard evidence that bubbles exist in the real world, or are we just playing a game of logic?

CHAPTER SIX

Attack of the Killer Anomalies

SHAREHOLDER: *(still standing in the bubblescope room):* *Now that we have this massive contraption, I suppose we can accomplish something. Tell me, Mr. Bubblescope, what are the first signs of a bubble?*

PHILOSOPHER: *The first thing that sets off bubble alarms is the presence of something truly puzzling, a pattern that shouldn't be there, a price that defies simple analysis.*

SHAREHOLDER: *What do you look for next?*

PHILOSOPHER: *The next thing I do is look again. In many ways, finance is like quantum physics. The actions of an observer affect the events being observed. Often, as soon as some researcher finds a strange pattern, it disappears. The act of identifying the phenomenon extinguished it. A bubble pattern should not disappear.*

SHAREHOLDER: *Can you give me an example?*

PHILOSOPHER: *Certainly. Look at this set of bubblescope observations. Ten years ago, we calculated the average return for the stock market on each day of the week. In a purely random world, the return should be the same each day. For every period we could find, however, there was a striking pattern. Monday was always the worst day. It was as if a tiny bubble formed on many, many Fridays and popped on the subsequent Mondays. Let me tell you—when this news crossed my desk, I was excited.*

SHAREHOLDER: *What happened next? Did anyone have an explanation?*

PHILOSOPHER: *Look at this next set of observations. After the pattern became public knowledge, it disappeared! Arbitrageurs drove it away.*

SHAREHOLDER: *So it was a bubble!*

PHILOSOPHER: *I prefer to think not. A bubble is something that we know shouldn't happen but does anyway—and repeatedly. The market is not God. It can factor in only things that humans know. Nobody bothered to look for the Monday effect, so the market never adjusted for it. Once it was observed, everything changed.*

SHAREHOLDER: *Does every oddity disappear once it is known?*

PHILOSOPHER: *Not quite. Remember: As soon as we know something is true about the market, it ceases to be. Which is, of course, true about that statement as well!*

SHAREHOLDER: *You're talking in circles. Either the statement is true or it isn't.*

PHILOSOPHER: *The question isn't what I as the philosopher believe about the market, but what investors and traders believe. At times throughout history, everyone appeared to believe in efficient markets—times when faith in the markets was practically universal. Exactly during those times strange things often happened. Looking there, we have found weird anomalies that persist. Perhaps the strangest is this: Unanimity precedes crashes.*

SHAREHOLDER: *If we now know that we should be especially cautious when we are unanimously confident, shouldn't even that effect go away?*

PHILOSOPHER: *Perhaps, but it hasn't yet.*

One of the oldest methods used by bubble seekers is the search for strange anomalies. The first and most famous of these was Tulipmania. Over the years, and especially since the early 1980s, the number of documented freakish price movements has skyrocketed.

One of the most striking recent anomalies is the tendency for stock returns to be negative on Mondays. For many years, no one bothered to look for a pattern in stock market returns on a particular day of the week. Those first calculations amazed researchers. The return on Mondays was extraordinary. Between 1928 and 1987, Monday was the worst day to be in the stock market for every five-year period. If returns were truly random across days, the chance of observing the historical Monday effect would be less than one in a billion. For sixty years, outperforming an investment in a simple index fund would have been a snap—something the efficient-market mavens believed should be impossible—simply by selling on Friday and buying on Tuesday.

Other irregularities abound. Returns have tended to be higher in January; the effect is too regular to be chalked up to simple chance. Until recently at least, January has been the best month almost every year. And not just the calendar appears to matter. The market has tended to outperform in years that the National Football Conference champion wins the Super Bowl. The four worst-performing stocks in the Dow Jones Industrial Index, the so-called Dogs of the Dow, have posted

higher returns than other firms in the Dow almost every
year.

While the number of potential anomalies is enormous, the significance of most of them is highly questionable, at least to efficient-market believers. Perhaps
billions of possible variables could explain the stock market. Over time, observations can rule many out. But given
the large population of candidates, coincidences can still
occur. In a billion trials, a one-in-a-billion event can easily happen.

What makes an anomaly scientifically interesting?
Persistence is the most important characteristic. Coincidences often crop up in history. An irregularity becomes
important when its finder can make gobs of money by
exploiting it. Anomalies, at least the widely reported ones,
have a poor track record in making money. Just after
everyone in finance began puzzling over the Monday
effect, it disappeared. Since the Monday effect was first
reported, the opposite has been true. Mondays have been
the best day of the week! After the Dogs-of-the-Dow
investment strategy became popular, it stopped working.

After decades of research, the stock market anomalies
can be divided into three distinct categories. The first is
the set of apparent anomalies—such as the effect of the
Super Bowl winner—that are coincidences. No rational
explanation exists for the observed correlation. The second group is the anomalies that have a plausible logical
cause but are blatant enough for arbitrageurs to undo the
anomaly easily once it is recognized. The Monday effect
may reflect the fact that busy shareholders in need of
money arrange their affairs before a sale over the week-
end and then place their sell order Monday mornings.
Once market participants know that many investors

behave in that way, they can react and profit from that behavior until the effect is no longer observable in prices. The January effect may have lasted for many years because of the regular repurchase of shares that had been sold at the end of the previous year for tax purposes. Cognizant of the pattern, traders can profit until their activities make the puzzling pattern go away—and appear to have done so.

One intriguing set of anomalies does challenge efficient-market theories. In this third group we find puzzling patterns in the data that are perhaps best explained by an appeal to predictable behavior under ambiguous circumstances. Some researchers have used behavioral constants to produce testable implications for the stock market. A significant set of anomalies often supports their theories. Most important, unlike the second set of anomalies, these persist even after scholars identify them. For some reason arbitrageurs can't trade the anomalies into oblivion.

Why does the third type persist? As discussed in chapter 5, when ambiguity surrounds us, we all rely partly on clues drawn from the actions and statements of our fellow travelers. As social animals, our ability to interpret others has been honed over thousands of years. If that caveman next to you thinks the twig snap signals the approach of a saber-toothed tiger, you are more likely to draw the same inference. Each of us has a stock of experiences that provides independent insights. Perhaps the person next to you knows something that you don't. Tigers may hunt more often at night in the fall. They may be attracted to a nearby salt lick that you didn't know about. Reliance on others is a natural and logical product of evolutionary forces. If we can quickly recognize the value of the opinions of others and adjust our own in response, a group of humans can collectively access far more information and intellectual firepower than any individual can.

One of the great challenges of economic life is knowing what you need to know. Sometimes you don't fully understand a situation because nobody does. Sometimes you don't fully understand a situation because you are less informed than others. In finance, the stock market combines the wisdom of others. If the price of a particular stock is higher today, someone somewhere must have decided to buy the stock. This aspect of the stock market may interact with the tools that evolution gave us to deal with ambiguity so that wider price swings occur than the fluctuation of fundamentals alone cause. And those swings may lead to the smoking-gun anomalies discussed next.

Suppose you decide to take another look at Internet stocks. Let's use Amazon.com as an example. With the price beaten down after the collapse of the Internet sector, the stock might seem promising. Should you buy? You might start by analyzing the fundamentals. How high did sales climb? Have they been growing? Is the company making money? Suppose that your analysis doesn't lead to a decisive answer. The current market price for the company is much higher than justified by information in currently observable fundamentals.

Should you give up and purchase some other stock? Maybe. But the future of the company might be more promising than analysis of the current basics implies. Events beyond our historical experience might be lurking around the corner. Amazon.com might take over the retail world and earn mountains of profits. Part of you, perhaps the part that enjoys shopping online, thinks that the firm may conquer the world. Another part remembers the sorry fate of those who invested in dot-coms in the late 1990s.

Add another factor to the equation. Suppose that the price of Amazon.com starts climbing a bit each day. It is selling for $5 per share. Suppose that a week from now the price is $6. A week after that it is $7, then $9. What impact will those events have on your beliefs about the company's prospects? If you are like most people, you will become more optimistic. The increasing price suggests a decision by many other market participants that the company is solid, just as your online-shopping self always believed. Since those new buyers might be better informed than you, it is perfectly reasonable to become more optimistic, too.

Under those circumstances, the price of Amazon.com might increase for sensible reasons. People do learn, after all, from one another. But the same set of circumstances might signal a bubble. Suppose that a few analysts notice a small news item that leads them to adjust their outlook for Amazon.com favorably. If they purchase a healthy portion of stock, the price of Amazon.com might increase a little. Next, several investors who were waffling about the purchase become more optimistic after seeing the price increase. They call their brokers and buy. That action puts further upward pressure on the price. The higher price causes even more investors to buy, and so on. The price has increased dramatically, far more than justified by the news that generated the surge. The original purchase started an avalanche of optimism because a sequence of investors used the price signal to make inferences about the information available to others. An evolutionarily sound inference strategy leads to faulty signal detection.

Fascinating recent contributions have identified specific phenomena that may be most consistent with those types of avalanches. While there is significant debate about the ultimate consequences of the phenomena, they have helped researchers focus their efforts in the right areas. Be forewarned, however. The efficient-market team has responses prepared for much of the work we are about to discuss. We will cover those responses in chapter 7.

AN OVERREACTION TO VALUE STOCKS?

The market processes so much information that it is difficult to verify any change in prices as a rational or irrational response to specific events. In the mid-1980s, two clever researchers thought of a test that might strongly suggest that buying and selling avalanches result from behavior that spreads like a virus from person to person. If true, then bubbles affect stock prices.

Researchers Werner F. M. DeBondt and Richard Thaler reasoned as follows: If positive price movements themselves beget other positive swings, one ought to observe overreaction to news. When there is good news about a company, the price should climb higher than justified by the news. With bad news, the price should drop more than pure rationality would predict.

Wait a minute, you're thinking. The sensitivity of pricing formulas should make such a test impossible. Perhaps the market understands the long-run impact of news better than our assumptions. That serious complaint was one of the main lessons of chapter 2, but DeBondt and Thaler thought of a clever way around it.

They observed a wide variation in the marketplace in the reward for a dollar's worth of earnings. Expensive stocks have high prices relative to their earnings, and cheap stocks have low prices relative to their earnings. A stock is cheap or expensive depending on the market's belief about a firm's prospects. If a firm is expected to go bankrupt soon—perhaps because it makes buggy whips that are about to go out of style—it may have healthy earnings today but a low stock price. If a firm is expected to become the hottest thing in town next year, its price today is high.

DeBondt and Thaler reasoned that firms with low prices relative to earnings are down on their luck. The efficient-market hypothesis argues that such firms are correctly priced at lower levels because of their poor prospects. Their future return, risk-adjusted, should be about that of the market as a whole. If on the other hand, irrational avalanches occurred, many firms acquired low prices relative to earnings because a bit of bad news started a panic. If the market overreacted to the bad news, firms with low prices should be buying opportunities, and portfolios of low-priced stocks might outperform other possible bundles of shares. That case would occur if true fundamentals ultimately won out, but extreme pessimism overpowers rationality in the short run following negative surprises.

In studies since replicated by others, DeBondt and Thaler found exactly that pattern in the data. Portfolios of value stocks, with low prices relative to earnings, earned high returns relative to comparable market portfolios. A recent example of just such a stock is Tidewater, the oil-service firm. In late 1997, the share price stood at $60. Then oil prices dropped sharply and market participants became very pessimistic about Tidewater's future. Why would U.S. suppliers bother to drill new oil wells with prices that low? The price of Tidewater plummeted below $18. At that low price, the firm still had solid earnings, since the pessimistic scenario had yet to play out. The price-to-earnings (P/E) ratio for Tidewater was as low as 3, about one-eighth that of the market as a whole. Subsequently, things were not as bad as the market feared, and the share price doubled between 1999 and 2000.

Strong confirmation of the importance of overreactions came from another finding. Stocks with *high* prices tended to underperform other portfolios: Their performance suggests that the market overreacts to good news as well. Subsequently, researchers found similar results with other measures of high and low prices to identify winners and losers. Many researchers believe that the overreaction to news perfectly matches the predictions of avalanche models.

THE CLOSED-END PUZZLE

Many people own stocks through mutual funds. Almost everyone who does owns an open-end fund. The funds promise to invest your money in a specified set of assets, but the manager has a good deal of say about which specific stocks or bonds to own at any time. The amount of money invested by the fund is determined by the flows of cash in and out of the mutual fund. Successful funds, such as the Fidelity Magellan Fund, can acquire hundreds of billions of dollars in assets.

A closed-end fund is different. Far fewer investors

own them. A closed-end fund issues a fixed amount of shares; those are traded like stocks in the marketplace. To take money out of Fidelity Magellan, you issue a sell order; the company closes out your position at prices that hold at the end of the day. To take your money out of a closed-end fund, you have to find someone in the marketplace willing to purchase your shares.

Adams Express is one of the oldest closed-end funds. It, along with Wells Fargo and American Express, originally provided safe passage of financial documents between major metropolitan areas in the 1800s. Adams Express was the paymaster for both the Union and Confederate armies during the Civil War. As the U.S. Postal Service took on more and more delivery duties, the company had prudently invested its profits in a portfolio of blue-chip stocks. Beginning in 1873, individual investors could purchase a stake in that portfolio by acquiring Adams Express stock. Those shares are still traded on the New York Stock Exchange (NYSE), although the portfolio today includes such firms as Cisco and Nokia.

Closed-end funds provide a wonderful laboratory for the study of efficient markets. Recall one of the major problems facing researchers in establishing whether the price the market sets for Johnson & Johnson (or any other stock) is right: There is so much uncertainty about what the right price might be. Small changes in assumptions about earnings growth can lead to dramatically different prices. We can readily see the right and rational price for closed-end funds. A fund is nothing more than a bundle of shares of stocks. If those stocks are publicly traded, we can use the market's estimate of the value of the shares to construct a fully rational price.

Suppose that a closed-end fund—let's call it the Topridge Fund—owns ten shares of Johnson & Johnson and ten shares of Amazon.com. Assume that the price of Johnson & Johnson shares is $50 per share; the total value of the shares is $500. The price of Amazon.com is $5 per share, with a total value of $50. Since the fund holds both bundles, the total value of the Topridge fund should be $550. Once we know that, we can easily construct a test of market efficiency. If one share of the Topridge Fund is traded in the marketplace, its price had better be $550!

Researchers have studied the prices of closed-end funds for decades. Several startling regularities have emerged. Most important, Harvard economist Andrei Shleifer and his coauthors have developed a model of investor behavior that demonstrates that the pattern is indicative of the presence of fools. Shleifer calls fools "noise traders," and his model that includes them accurately predicts subtle nuances that can be observed in closed-end prices.

Shleifer observed four regularities. First, closed-end funds usually start out trading at a premium compared with the value of the shares held by the fund. The Topridge Fund might trade at about $600 at the outset. Second, the premium usually disappears in a matter of months. Funds that are more than a year old typically sell at discounts to their fundamental value; those discounts can be enormous. The average discount is 10 to 20 percent. If our Topridge Fund is typical, it will be worth about $500 a year later, rather than the fundamental value of $550 months after being issued. Third, the discounts swing over time and add a risk to individual shareholders that is not present if they buy the individual shares themselves. It is not uncommon for a discount to change 20 percent or more in a year. Finally, when closed-end funds are shut down or transformed into open-end funds, their value approaches their true fundamental value.

What could possibly explain such puzzling patterns? Shleifer and his coauthors argue that the most likely cause is the investors whose sentiment about the prospects of the closed-end funds depends on something other than fundamentals. An all-star manager with a solid record of outperforming the marketplace decides to start up a closed-end fund, for example. If markets are efficient, some managers through luck will always manage to outperform the stock market. Those who outperformed the market yesterday will not be expected to outperform it tomorrow. Noise-trading investors don't know that. They rush to invest in the star's new enterprise and buy closed-end shares at a premium. Over time the investors' faith in the manager fluctuates as traders become more or less convinced that he is as good as his record indicates. Since the fluctuation in sentiment makes the closed-end fund riskier than a simple portfolio of the same stocks, the fund must ultimately trade at a discount.

Shleifer's model of investor sentiment masterfully explains those and other price patterns. The weird patterns have continued after being recognized. Arbitrage is not so powerful that it can sweep away the effects of sentiment.

ANOTHER PUZZLE

Another puzzle involves the S&P 500 index. The index is a set of five hundred firms chosen by Standard & Poor's as a sample of the entire U.S. stock market. Open-end mutual funds that invest in a bundle of stocks designed to match the index have become the investment of choice for investors who believe in market efficiency, generally because the simple index funds have outperformed other actively managed funds by a large margin.

An S&P announcement that a new stock will be added to the index generates a remarkable event. The price of the stock rises significantly and strangely. Unlike an earnings announcement, inclusion in the index is not a traditionally newsworthy event for a firm. One recent study that analyzed the twenty-year period between 1976 and 1996 found that the price increase averaged 3.5 percent following an announcement. And the effect persisted even after the news became public knowledge. In September 2001 the pharmaceutical company Immunex was added to the index; its share price jumped from $16.37 to $18.15, almost an 11 percent gain. Those jumps suggest that prices move for reasons other than news about fundamentals and challenge the efficient-market theories.

What could explain those patterns? There are several candidates. Many mutual funds that use an index strategy are forced to purchase shares in a newcomer after the announcement. The surge in buy orders might lead to the jump in price. This is the most commonly held explanation. An alternative is required, however, because the price movement tends to continue. The demand effect alone should cause a temporary spike in price, followed by a return to the true fundamental value. Since the price increase does not reverse itself, something lasting about a company changes when included in the index. The most likely reason the inclusion leads to a permanent price increase is that it signals to investors that Standard & Poor's has decided that the particular firm has made it and become an established part of American life. In a world of ambiguous decision making, the belief of such an august body logically affects the beliefs of investors.

The observation is easily cast in terms of our resident philosopher's simple conceptual model of ambiguity. Think of the American economy as an expanding universe. Some firms exist safely in the interior; some prospect at the frontiers, where ambiguity is greatest. The prospectors must offer investors a high expected return because the ambiguity at the frontier is so high and investors abhor ambiguity. Standard & Poor's announcement to the world that a firm is in the index signals that the frontier has moved beyond the company. The firm is now safely entrenched in the interior of the bubble sphere as an integral part of economic life. Investors respond by permanently becoming more willing to invest in that company's shares.

IS NO NEWS GOOD NEWS?

The next set of results perhaps tested the efficient-market view most directly. Think back to why the market price of a stock is a random walk in theory. The price today is based on a forward-looking and rational guess about the future circumstances of a firm. If the price changes tomorrow, there must have been some news about the firm. But if investors search each other for clues about the direction of prices, prices may move for no apparent reason.

An attempt to pinpoint the exact case could logically proceed in one of two ways. First, we could investigate the impact that trading itself might have on the movement of stock prices up and down. The task is relatively easy because the market occasionally closes for unrelated reasons such as holidays. If price swings are exaggerated, trading itself increases the volatility of stocks. We can detect that increase easily. Suppose that the market occasionally closes on Tuesdays. If we compare the average movement from Monday to Wednesday for share prices when the market is open on Tuesday with the same movement when the market is closed on Tuesday, we can estimate the impact of trading on prices. The exercise, performed several times, has clear results. Prices tend to swing much more between Monday and Wednesday if the market reopens on the Tuesday in between. The result is suggestive but not decisive. There may be less news when the market is closed. Many folks who ordinarily gather news might have the day off.

The second approach is far more challenging, but more promising as well. Suppose that we observe a share price over time and find that it moved sharply on just a few days. Thorough research might be able to find an explanation for those movements. Was there a major news story about the firm the day that its share price shot up? If so, the movement was consistent with the efficient-market view. If a thorough search of all possible news sources can't find anything that could remotely explain the great price swing, the markets did not respond to news at all but dropped for no good reason.

The 1987 stock market crash was one of the first events subjected to enough intense scrutiny to provide intriguing evidence. The Dow Jones Industrial Average dropped almost 23 percent on October 19, its largest one-day decline ever. Particularly puzzling about the day, nothing could be found to justify the decline: no news of war, no massive earnings disappointment. Economist Robert Shiller mailed one thousand questionnaires to institutional investors and two thousand to individuals on October 19, just after the crash. Among other things, he asked for individual theories about the crash. Most responded that they thought the market had been over-priced. That response is hardly a solid piece of news. But did a short-term irrational panic lead to the decline? It may be as good a theory as any.

One anecdote does not make a convincing case. David Cutler, James Poterba, and Lawrence Summers attempted to gather significant enough data to justify more sweeping conclusions. They sifted through the data for the fifty greatest movement days in stock market his-tory and then hit the library to identify the news event that led to the big day. They pored over the *New York Times* for the cause reported for the large swing. They also investi-gated whether something missed was a plausible cause of the swing. On September 3, 1946, the stock market dropped almost 7 percent, a massive drop. The *Times* could find "no basic reason for the assault on prices." On June 29, 1962, the market soared almost 3.5 percent. According to the *Times,* "Stock prices advanced strongly chiefly because they had gone down so long and so far that a rally was due." On November 30, 1982, the market again soared more than 3 percent. "Analysts were at a loss to explain why the Dow jumped so dramatically in the last two hours," reported the *Times.*

Sometimes the movements occurred because of an important change. On June 26, 1950, the market dropped almost 5.5 percent because of the outbreak of the Korean War. But most large movements had no identifiable cause. If news about fundamentals moves stock prices, the big moves should coincide with big news. What's most star-tling is the quiet that accompanies large movements in the stock market. No matter how hard researchers dig, they often can find no explanation for great prices swings. Jeremy Siegel concluded that "when reviewing the causes of major market movements, it is sobering to realize that less than one-quarter can be associated with a news event of major political or economic import."

What should we make of his conclusion? The inability to find news logically leading to large price swings that we observed may be attributable to the inadequacies of the researchers. If the stock market were super-efficient, like the Borg Collective, it might well process information far more complex and subtle than the average newspaper reporter could identify. Sensible movements that depend on a vast constellation of minute influences would appear mysterious. The high count of unexplained movement days, however, is broadly consistent with other evidence gathered in this chapter. Something besides earnings and interest rates affects stock prices. But what?

PHYSICISTS TO THE RESCUE!

Oxford physics professor Neil F. Johnson and his colleagues may have found the answer. Johnson is a condensed-matter physicist. He has made a career of trying to model circumstances in which the behavior of the whole is quite different from the behavior of each part. At a historic meeting in Palermo in 1998, Johnson and his friends began discussing whether the tools that they were developing to study complex physical systems might have financial applications. The connection seemed promising precisely because of Siegel's observation. Markets appear to fluctuate because of some internal mechanism. Price swings are not always attributable to news. Johnson believed that the internal mechanism might be quite similar to a ball of physical particles.

The collaboration was so fruitful that Oxford recently endowed the Oxford Centre for Computational Finance and appointed faculty from the physics, mathematics, and computer science departments to coordinate its activities. In the three short years since the Palermo meeting, the authors have shed considerable light on the mechanism that may produce bubbles. Johnson and his colleagues observed that a market is made up of countless traders, each with a strategy for making money. Some investors may follow momentum strategies and load up on stocks that have just increased in price. Others may believe in overreaction and purchase shares that just went down. All traders tend to gravitate toward strategies that have been successful recently.

The Oxford model was built on the observation that it is possible—with a powerful enough computer—to construct a market universe inhabited by virtual traders—computer programs designed to reproduce real-world trading strategies. The ingenious innovation was this: The Oxford scientist could run the simulation backward and identify at any time what the true population's trading strategies must look like, given recently observed swings in share prices. The researchers then asked, "Do patterns in the trading strategies help predict large price swings in the market?" They have found powerful evidence that they do.

The Oxford model has successfully predicted periods of extreme volatility, including the 1987 stock market crash. Amazingly, the model relied upon only information that was available prior to the crash. The dangerous periods are intervals when agents all agree with each other about the most profitable trading strategy. The calm before the storm masks extreme instability because bits of information that undermine the traders' faith in a given strategy can trigger an avalanche away from it, an avalanche that hits frontier-dwelling firms the hardest. The model predicts that risk is lowest when traders all disagree with each other about the correct strategy.

The authors also developed superstrategies using information contained in the strategies of traders to determine when to buy and when to sell. In one simulation, a superstrategy focusing on currency markets returned 380 percent between 1990 and 1999. Such an enormous return clearly challenges efficient markets. What would happen if traders begin to use superstrategies? The Oxford physicists believe that they can include superstrategies in their model and attempt to isolate profitable super-superstrategies. After those are digested by the market, the development of super-super-superstrategies would be necessary. The evolution of their efforts could be one of the most intriguing financial developments to follow over the next decade.

THE FINAL PIECE OF THE PUZZLE

The last bit of evidence that challenges efficiency is known as the *equity premium puzzle.* Its impact on the debate, while subtle, is crucial. The efficient-market model predicts that an asset should give a fair and reasonable return commensurate with the amount of risk that it forces you to take on. The equity premium puzzle is fairly easy to state: Why do stocks put so much more money in people's pockets over time than bonds and other assets? The size of the puzzle is extraordinary. As mentioned earlier, if you had invested $2,000 in the stock market in 1950, by 2000 its value would have grown to almost $1.2 million. But if you had invested that money in long-term government bonds, the stake would have grown to a measly $25,000. The puzzle is especially important because it involves the stock market as a whole, not a small subset of closed-end funds or a narrow slice of big movement days.

Some researchers have attempted to explain the puzzle with models of risk. Individuals dislike wild swings in the prices of the assets that they own, and hate being presented with the chance of losing all their money. They should demand a higher expected return when asked to invest in a shaky scheme. These models measure the risk of different assets by their historical volatility. If a stock has swung wildly, it is considered risky. If its price has been fairly stable, it is said to be a *safe haven.*

In practice, the attempts to explain high stock market returns or even patterns of returns across different firms with traditional risk measures have been unsuccessful. Stocks are not nearly risky enough—at least if volatility measures risk—to explain the enormous extra historical return from holding them. Bonds may have highly volatile prices over time, but the circumstances of most bonds are highly unambiguous. If inflation and interest rates soar, your bond is worth less.

The prospects of a stock are highly ambiguous, and individuals often are strongly averse to ambiguity. The aversion may explain why they have historically shied away from stocks even more than their volatility predicts. Ellsberg's paradox, which suggests that humans shy away from circumstances in which they don't have enough information to go on, may be the best explanation of the puzzle.

While the findings presented here have often with-stood heated counterattacks, the debate over bubbles continues to this day. As we will see in chapter 7, many of the bizarre phenomena identified here may have rational explanations. Those few that do not, however, provide important clues to prudent investors about the types of circumstances that are most foreboding.

CHAPTER SEVEN

Revenge of the Nerds

SHAREHOLDER: *This bubblescope room is boiling! What's wrong?*

PHILOSOPHER: *It's probably the supercomputers. They generate an enormous amount of heat.*

SHAREHOLDER: *What do you use them for?*

PHILOSOPHER: *We couldn't launch a serious search without them. After the scope identifies a candidate bubble, we enter all relevant information into the computer. The computer spins, sifts, and searches for any possible explanation of our observations. If there is one, the bubble has been garberred, and we file it away as a false alarm.*

SHAREHOLDER: *What?!*

PHILOSOPHER: *Garberred. We call it that because the first and greatest bubble debunker was a fellow named Peter Garber. A garberred event has been explained. We haven't found a bubble—we've found only a complex but rational event.*

SHAREHOLDER: *How often do you find a good explanation?*

PHILOSOPHER: *Almost always.*

SHAREHOLDER: *You can't be serious!*

PHILOSOPHER: *I am quite serious. Go ahead—try me. Pick an event. I'll focus my machine on it.*

SHAREHOLDER: *OK, how about Tulipmania. Tulip bulbs were selling for $50,000 apiece four hundred years ago! That must have been a bubble.*

PHILOSOPHER: *Not quite $50,000, but you are close. Tulipmania, however, was most certainly not a bubble! That was one of Garber's first contributions.*

SHAREHOLDER: *Go on.*

PHILOSOPHER: *Let's turn the scope to the problem.*

[The philosopher hits a knob on the bubblescope. The economic universe shrinks dramatically. The year reads 1638. On the edge of the giant sphere, the scope zooms in on an auction in Amsterdam. Men are bidding for a bulb held aloft by the auctioneer.]

SHAREHOLDER: *See—that little onion-like bulb just sold for 5,500 guilders. That's almost 110 ounces of gold!*

PHILOSOPHER: *It's an impressive price—and it should be. That bulb is a Semper Augustus. Its flower is one of the most beautiful ever seen.*

SHAREHOLDER: *But that can't be a reasonable price! The poor fellow is going to lose everything. Let's fast-forward and see how it turns out.*

[The Philosopher spins the knobs and the date reads 1738. He focuses the bubblescope on a tiny garden shop in Amsterdam, well in the interior of the economic sphere.]

PHILOSOPHER: *This shop is selling a large bundle of Semper Augustus bulbs for 5 guilders.*

SHAREHOLDER: *I knew it! Now you can purchase a bucket*

full of bulbs at a fraction of the auction price. That poor fool lost everything. The bulb is now worthless.

PHILOSOPHER: *On the contrary, that "poor" man is quite rich. And all because of his daring purchase of a Semper Augustus.*

SHAREHOLDER: *How can that be?*

PHILOSOPHER: *When he purchased the bulb, it was a rare mutation, the only one of its kind. Our entrepreneur believed that he could sell the bulbs to all of Holland because of their beauty. He did succeed eventually—but tulips reproduce slowly. Our man in Amsterdam planted the bulb; a year later he had two. He planted those and reaped more the next year, and so on. Only after twenty years did he have enough to commercialize. A hundred years later, hundreds of thousands of bulbs sold for a small amount, but the total profits were impressive. Some of the wealthiest families in Holland owe their wealth in part to Tulipmania.*

SHAREHOLDER: *Then why was it called a bubble?*

PHILOSOPHER: *Historians later saw the sharp drop in prices and concluded that the worst had happened. But the pattern is common. Tulip prices show the same pattern today.*

SHAREHOLDER: *I'm beginning to enjoy this bubblescope. Let's turn it to the dot-coms.*

PHILOSOPHER: *In a moment. But first, an experiment I've always wanted to perform. Legend has it that a millionaire's houseguest thought that a priceless tulip bulb was an onion—and ate it. I've always wondered about that.*

[He pulls out a tulip bulb.]

SHAREHOLDER: *I want the first bite!*

While the evidence in chapters 5 and 6 is highly suggestive, it by no means proves that bubbles exist. Just as the original literature about the random walk led to an ener-

getic search for counterexamples and differences, the
flurry of anomalies produced an aggressive counterattack
by efficient-market enthusiasts. Those parries have at
times been effective—so effective that as many economists still believe in efficient markets as not. If you followed the media storm surrounding the collapse of the
share prices of many dot-coms, you might think that only
hopeless nerds could still have faith in the working of the
markets. But their case is far from hopeless, with significant implications for investors. Advocates of the efficient
market have provided bubble searchers a valuable service.
After the dust settled, a small but significant subset of the
bubble evidence survives. The results point out where to
look and what to look for when deciding whether price
increases are sensible or attributable to bubbles.

A main shortcoming of behavioral finance—and the
bubble sightings of its devotees—is that the appearance
of irrationality may only be a by-product of a feckless
attempt to define the rational. A giant of behavioral finance, Richard Thaler, presents an interesting case. He set
out to study the behavior of taxi drivers. Thaler believed
that they—like all humans—might not behave like Vulcan
superrational beings, and he suggested an ingenuous
experiment.

Taxi drivers normally spend much of their time driving
an empty taxi as they look for customers. But on rainy days
customers increase, and profits are higher. Thaler argued
that a Vulcan taxi driver would work long hours on rainy
days since the reward for an extra hour was so high. But a
human is a creature of habit. An individual might well drive
the same number of hours as usual, even in bad weather.

The professor fastidiously gathered data on actual
driver behavior and didn't find much evidence that taxi

drivers behaved optimally. If anything, they drove shorter hours on rainy days. Thaler concluded that the cabbies behaved in odd suboptimal ways and that any scientific model of their actions must account for psychological factors. Many researchers still consider Thaler's work a decisive challenge to the view that actions of rational agents drive the markets. Countless other scholars have adopted his approach.

But does the evidence argue against rationality? Charles Calomiris, an economist at Columbia University, recently demonstrated to me how fragile such analysis can be. He went to the source. He got into a taxi in New York City and described Thaler's results to the driver. Then he asked the driver to comment. Did he drive more or less on rainy days? Was the cabdriver acting because of habit or emotion instead of reason?

The driver agreed with the empirical evidence. He always drove fewer hours on rainy days. But he argued that his actions were fully rational, and he was indignant (in a manner only a New Yorker can muster) that anyone would suggest otherwise. Wet roads are much more treacherous, with a greater chance of accident. Three accidents in a year would cause a cabbie to lose his right to drive a taxi!

After that conversation, I reread Thaler's paper. Sure enough, there was no reference to accidents. Perhaps drivers were not so irrational after all. Perhaps Thaler was the one making a mistake. In any case, it would be quite entertaining to see him defend the research before Calomiris's driver.

The important lesson is often ignored. Incomplete characterization of a problem can lead to a false identification of anomalies. After all, everything about markets is strange to a child. Close inspection suggests that many smoking-gun anomalies make more sense than we might think.

BIG LOSERS, BIG COMEBACKS, BIG RISKS?

Thaler found that firms with low prices relative to fundamentals outperform other companies. Those seeking psychological explanations for the behavior of the stock market rely on those key foundations. A variation of the result was Robert Shiller's key motivation for writing *Irrational Exuberance.* He found that high price-to-earnings (P/E) ratios preceded periods of market gloom; he attributed that circumstance to investor psychology. This pattern created an apparently effective trading strategy: Sell when the P/E is high. An efficient market should allow no such thing.

Possible answers crop up in different places. University of Chicago economist Eugene Fama and his co-author, Kenneth French, argue that the pattern itself makes sense. Firms with high fundamental risk *should* have a low market value relative to fundamentals. But to compensate shareholders for the risk, the shaky companies should offer a higher expected return. The anomalous result should be expected in a well-functioning market!

The factor may seem surprising since most investors (and some professors) assume that high P/E stocks are more risky. But the opposite is true. Suppose that two companies—Mary's Speedboats and Anne's Speedboats—have identical fundamentals. Both have current earnings of $1 million and identical long-run prospects. What price should the market assign the two companies? If everything is the same, the prices should be the same. But what happens if there is one small difference? Suppose that Mary is an unstable person who might run off to Bermuda with the company's money. Anne is a respectable churchgoer. Which firm has the higher stock market price? Obviously Anne's. Investors penalize Mary for the risk associated with her character. Companies with low prices relative to fundamentals are riskier, and they must offer a higher expected return to compensate shareholders. The relationship does not threaten market efficiency at all. If anything, it powerfully confirms that the market works wonders.

Another problem with the ability of P/E ratios to predict earnings is that the relationship itself is far less trustworthy than it appears at first glance. That characteristic was driven home to me in early 2000 when I traveled to Florida to debate Robert Shiller about the future of the stock market. Having just read his *Irrational Exuberance,* I was struck by a potential problem with his analysis. Shiller's entire argument rested on the observation that high P/E ratios signaled that you should sell stocks. But his case had a major flaw.

False bubble profits have repeated the error many times. Shiller gathered P/E ratios for many years and observed that the market tended to underperform after the ratio was high and overperform after the ratio was low. In 1996, with the Dow hovering at about 6,000, the relationship motivated him to testify at the Federal Reserve that a major correction was due. Events did not conform to his predictions—and they shouldn't have. His error was simple. Since price is part of P/E, his relationship would likely have held no matter what variable he related the stock market price to. A price above its long-run historical average must be expected to decline simply because it is above the average. Similarly, if a historical series is

below its long-run average, it will generally be expected
to increase. The average is, after all, the best guess from
a historical series. If we could travel in a time machine
back to 1950 and tell investors what the average P/E will
be between 1950 and 2000, they could make money on
the information! We are giving them information that they
couldn't possibly ever have—knowledge about the average P/E in the future!

Back in the real world, we do not know in 2001 what
the average P/E will be between 2002 and 2050. How
might Shiller have constructed a relationship that could
benefit the investor? Suppose that we use the average historical P/E up to 1949 to devise a trading rule that
depends on the data. One simple rule would be to purchase stocks if the P/E is below the long-run average but
to purchase bonds if the P/E is above the long-run average. The investor could try again in 1951 and change his
investment depending on the average P/E up to 1950. If
the P/E rule has any value, trading on the information
between 1950 and today should produce high profits. The
strategy should work in real time.

In preparation for the debate with Shiller, I let a hypo-
thetical investor adopt the P/E trading rule and compared
his return between 1950 and 2000 with his gain from putting his money in the market and letting it ride. The buy-
and-hold strategy beat the P/E rule by about a factor of
about ten!

In a gracious response, Shiller (ever the delightful
gentleman) correctly responded that the particular trading
strategy was not his rule, but he didn't give a substitute
that performed any better. Nothing overturns the observation that the ability of fundamental ratios to predict future
stock returns is striking only when looking backward. The

observation has not been used to make money in a fair test and does not prove that panics and bubbles exist.

Subsequent (and independent) researchers have performed far more rigorous analyses of the fundamental ratios with similar results. In a thorough analysis of the ability of dividend-price ratios to predict high stock market returns, Amit Goyal and Ivo Welch, two economists at UCLA, found the dividend yield worthless for generating high trading returns. The value puzzle may just be a big mistake.

The final challenge to those results comes from Robert Hall's renowned Ely lecture, first mentioned in chapter 2. Hall asked himself why a P/E ratio might be high. An important factor would be the expectation of market participants that firms' earnings grow more than average. When Hall looked at specific dates, he found a striking correlation. High P/Es tended to precede periods with unusually high earnings growth; low P/Es tended to precede periods with lower-than-average earnings growth. The stock market has an uncanny ability to predict future earnings! The behavior of P/Es, to Hall at least, strongly supports the efficient-market view.

THE CLOSED-END PUZZLE REVISITED

You could argue that the evidence of closed-end funds backs market efficiency. The large premiums that appear as a new fund is issued are irrefutable evidence that some investors believe that a specific fund manager can outperform the market. The belief does not immediately refute the efficient-market hypothesis, however. As the early free-marketeers suggested, the market should discipline

unwise investors in the most painful way: They should lose
their money. Exactly that happens. Investors who paid
large premiums to let a star manager control their money
in a closed-end fund took a bath. The managers couldn't
outperform the market and saw the closed-end fund shares
trade at a discount to their true fundamental value. If bubbles exist, shouldn't we observe the opposite pattern?
Shouldn't all-star managers regularly make enormous
profits and charge equally impressive fees to their clients?

Large discounts may reflect investors' belief that a
fund is especially risky. Such risk might include the possibility that management will raise expense ratios.
Recently, researchers found that the market capitalizes
risk correctly into share prices. Closed-end funds with
large discounts offered higher returns than funds with low
discounts. The market rationally prices the relative risk of
even closed-end funds. The existence of the closed-end
funds depends on the presence of dupes. The market's
subsequent pricing of the funds is rational.

A problem remains. How do we explain the large premiums at the initiation of the fund? Trading is so relatively thin that the significance of the premium is
questionable. The stakes are so low that hedge funds and
other arbitrageurs shy away from attempts to trade the
anomalous premiums away. Finally—and most important—if the closed-end fund premiums were truly an
anomalous moneymaking opportunity, new funds should
be introduced at higher and higher rates to take advantage
of the enormous profit potential. You should put the book
down this instant and go start one!

Are you still here? That's because the opposite has
been the case. New closed-end fund sightings are about as
common as those of Bigfoot. While suckers are born

every day, they don't come with pockets filled with cash—they lost theirs already. Experienced investors have learned to be wary of closed-end funds.

THE EQUITY PREMIUM PUZZLE

In *Dow 36,000,* my coauthor, James K. Glassman, and I argued that the historical equity premium was high because there hadn't been any research on the relative safety of stocks over the long run. As researchers discovered that stocks were less risky over longer periods, the message spread to shareholders. They then became more willing to purchase stocks, and this bid up prices. Where might the process logically lead? If everyone fully digested and believed the academic research suggesting that stocks are not very risky in the long run, then the Dow Jones Industrial Average would immediately jump to around 36,000. While such a dramatic occurrence is unlikely, it does suggest that those who have argued that the recent market surge is attributable to irrational causes have not made a convincing case. Author Mark Smith remarked on the importance that this logic has in the debate over market bubbles in his fabulous book *Toward Rational Exuberance.* There he wrote, "Behavioralist bears like Shiller do more than simply argue that the bulls are wrong. They say, in effect, that the bulls are 'irrational' . . . Whatever one thinks of the case made by bulls such as Abby Joseph Cohen, James Glassman, and Kevin Hassett, however, their arguments are certainly not irrational. If these arguments themselves are not inherently irrational, why is it that investors who accept this reasoning are presumed to be acting irrationally?"

People have also learned several other lessons. Forty years ago, many thought that a good broker got you in and out of the market at just the right time. Today virtually everyone recognizes that trying to time the market is fruitless. "Buy and hold" has become etched in the consciousness of individuals.

As investors have learned those lessons, their willingness to own stocks has bid up prices. Higher prices are not necessarily great news. Now that stocks are more expensive, the expected return is lower. How much lower? Jeremy Siegel, author of the important *Stocks for the Long Run,* recently told readers of the *New York Times* that the correction is almost complete. Equities will no longer outperform bonds. Glassman and I believe that there is still a little room and that stocks will likely outperform bonds by a few percentage points. But almost everyone agrees that the gradual increase in the willingness to own stocks has boosted share prices in recent years. As a test of market efficiency, the evolution in the equity premium rules out the extreme efficiency that appealed to early free-marketeers. If the market were as omniscient as God, then there would be nothing to learn. Prices in 1950 would already reflect scientific findings discovered in the 1980s. If the market learns over time, was it irrational in the past? If we adjust the definition of *efficiency* to state that the market incorporates all information known to humans when the price is set, efficiency holds up just fine.

Two economists have proposed an alternative explanation for the equity premium puzzle. William Goetzmann and Philippe Jorion's evidence suggests that there is no equity premium puzzle at all. The crucial error of previous studies is the intense focus on the U.S. stock market. If the analyses include other stock markets in existence in the twentieth century, the case for equities with an extraordinarily high return is much weaker. Of the thirty-nine countries studied by Goetzmann and Jorion, the United States had the highest equity returns by far. Many stock markets of the twentieth century experienced catastrophic events—some even disappeared. Looking only at the U.S. market can be, they argue, completely misleading.

Their case is solid. The market is a random battlefield with big winners and big losers every year. Focusing on half the equation can indeed lead to false conclusions.

The high U.S. equity returns could well be a statistical fluke, but there is another possibility. Perhaps the United States possesses an economic and political system uniquely qualified to generate prosperity, and other countries are only now beginning to emulate it. In that case, the experience of the U.S. market in the twentieth century is a solid indicator of the possibilities for the world in the twenty-first century, and focusing on the United States is the best strategy.

Once again the arguments on all sides are strong. The equity premium puzzle fizzles as a reliable bubble indicator.

WHAT'S LEFT?

Several important directions of inquiry have survived counterattack, and they suggest that a reliable warning indicator may well be within our grasp.

Since the anomalies presented in chapter 6 are almost all the scientific evidence in this area, we must conclude that the case for the existence of bubbles is incomplete. But the belief in an omniscient market, fully and perfectly peering into the future and setting prices honed to Olympian perfection, is likely gone forever. The market incorporates only available information. We learn in fits and starts; the market moves in a similar fashion as it wanders toward the price that an omniscient being might set. If you dig hard enough, you might outsmart the market. But in the end, news is public, and prices make sense.

David Cutler, James Poterba, and Lawrence Summers gave us intriguing evidence consistent with that view. Few remember that their study began with an attempt to explain the ups and downs of the market with fundamentals such as interest rates and the health of the economy. They found that their kitchen sink of factors explained only a small fraction of the ups and downs of the stock market. But their results produced a fascinating pattern. The three did poorly in explaining the monthly patterns of stock returns. Reasonable measures of fundamentals could explain only about 29 percent of the movement of stock prices; the rest, 71 percent, was attributable only to mysterious forces. When the economists tried to explain only annual movements in stock prices, their model could clarify 51 percent of the swings! They couldn't explain why the market goes up and down in the short run, but they could in the long run! It was as if you could not guess the whereabouts of a runner in five minutes but could pinpoint his position a year ahead.

The market, like the rest of us, progresses fitfully toward the truth. In the short run, different bits and pieces of the long-run puzzle appear daily, and the market processes those pieces as well as it can. If three bits of bad economic news indicate that the economy may be head-ing into a depression, the market flops. When other bits signal that the economy might not be so bad, the market recovers. In the end, how we are actually doing determines the ultimate path.

Some important deviations from absolute market perfection remain unchallenged. Prices can swing for undetectable reasons. Knightian uncertainty is undoubtedly present. When it is a major factor, odd things happen to trading and prices. Finally, information about the beliefs and strategies of those trading stocks appears to provide leading information about market crashes.

Bubbles are certainly possible—but they are like an animal with a strong smell. An odor suggests their presence, but we are still waiting for visual confirmation. And bubbles apparently cannot last long. At times we ask the market to perform the impossible: to price, in a sea of ambiguity, assets that exist at the frontier of our understanding. When we do, the connection between the prices that we observe and pure Vulcan reason is at its weakest. But as we gain knowledge, we correct mistakes quickly. In the meantime, an unwary investor can lose significant amounts of money, as many swept up in the high-tech rush of the 1990s found. Chapter 8 investigates whether these lessons can be used to develop a tool to provide an early warning of bubble events. And we test our own bubblescope to learn whether it would have predicted the dotcom crash.

CHAPTER EIGHT

Bubblespotting

[The investor and the philosopher are walking down a long flight of stairs.]

PHILOSOPHER: *Down here is the heart of our bubblescope operation. [Opens a door, revealing a room filled with hundreds of people—all in lab coats—watching television and reading newspapers and magazines.] When a bubble candidate survives our computer's attempt to be rationalized, we send it here to the bubbleologists.*

SHAREHOLDER: *Why are you using people, not machines?*

PHILOSOPHER: *The final bubble assessment depends on judgments that are too complex for a machine.*

SHAREHOLDER: *What judgments?*

PHILOSOPHER: *Once we think that we have spotted a possible bubble, we place that stock on a watch list. Our crack team of bubbleologists traces every piece of news about that firm and watches the share price closely. We are particularly interested in big swings in prices when there is no news about the company.*

SHAREHOLDER: *Somewhere there's something written about just about every firm. What do you call news?*

PHILOSOPHER: *That's still as much art as science. Sometimes a firm's shares tank because another firm in its industry warns that sales are down or because an executive leaves. Over time we have developed a system that accounts for the gray areas. Our bubbleologists are taught to classify news events according to a scale. On one end of the scale, our observer is sure that the news is significant; on the other end, the observer is sure that nothing was announced. If price movements repeatedly coincide with observations near the low end of the scale, the bubble siren goes off, and the event is sent next door for final validation.*

SHAREHOLDER: *Yet another room! Who does the final validation?*

PHILOSOPHER: *I'll show you. [They walk through a door with a sign that reads "Accountants Only!" Inside there are hundreds of people in lab coats watching television and reading newspapers.] Don't worry about the sign—I'm the boss.*

The people in this room are charged with watching old-economy firms deep in the interior of the economy and recording how their stock movements coincide with important events. If our candidate's behavior differs a lot from those in the control group, we have found a bubble.

SHAREHOLDER: *Why are there only accountants here?*

PHILOSOPHER: *They are the only ones who can stomach studying boring old companies for hours each day.*

SHAREHOLDER: *How often does something pass this final test?*

PHILOSOPHER: *So far we've had only one. Let me show you the file.*

The give-and-take of the warring financial scholars has shown that two related approaches have the most promise for bubble seekers. First, we now know that the financial system appears to generate variability itself without any inputs from external news events. The market fluctuates more when it is open than when it is closed. This may be because individuals base their beliefs about fundamentals in part on the beliefs of others and there is a good chance that buying and selling waves may occur under the right circumstances. Second, the search for news that accompanies major stock market movements has frequently been fruitless. Prices sometimes swing wildly for no identifiable reason. It's not the news that you see that signals trouble—it's the news that you don't!

Those two observations strongly challenge those efficient-market advocates who claim that the best investment strategy is to trust that the market has identified the correct and perfect price always and everywhere. Nonetheless, such trust has more often than not led to the best strategy—buy and hold. With few exceptions, bubble sightings have been about as reliable as those of the Loch Ness monster. Does the newest research mean that an individual investor could do (or at least sleep) better?

A SIMPLE STRATEGY FOR IDENTIFYING "GOOD" PRICE INCREASES

Suppose that you own a stock. Its share price just doubled. Has a bubble formed? Is it time to sell? Or did the price increase for good reasons? Either may be the case. A simple approach may allow an investor to separate the wheat from the chaff.

The key to identifying a good price increase is establishing whether some unexpected news could plausibly explain it. Sometimes share price movements make perfect sense. On October 23, 2001, the pharmaceutical company Pharmacia announced that sales of its highly profitable pain medication Celebrex would likely be lower than the firm had previously forecast. In response, the share price of Pharmacia dropped about 10 percent that day. At other times, it is more difficult to judge whether the share price movement is a rational response to news. When markets reopened the Monday after the terrorist attacks of September 11, 2001, the Dow Jones Industrial Average dropped 7 percent; Pharmacia dropped sharply as well. Were those declines a sensible response to the terrible news, correctly discounting the economic turmoil that would result from the terrorists actions, or was there a panic? It is almost impossible to judge. Finally, sometimes a share price moves for no apparent reason whatsoever. This last case is the one that most clearly indicates the possibility of bubbles, and it's this last case that we investigate closely in this chapter.

The market as a whole has always responded to factors that are difficult to assess, as it did during the 1987 crash, when share prices plunged for no apparent reason. Identifying bubble warnings by monitoring the extent to which *all stocks* respond to news is, therefore, not a promising investment strategy. Many of the most dramatic swings in the stock market over the past one hundred years occurred on days with little news. Over that period, an investor who purchased and held on to stocks earned a tremendous return. Simply steering clear of the market as a whole because its fluctuations appeared puzzling would have been a foolish strategy. This association has quite optimistic implications. Perhaps the normal state of economic affairs is that the economy grows and citizens prosper. Only when bad news interrupts calm does the market turn sour.

The events that followed the terrorist attacks of September 11 are an interesting case in point. The market recovered the lost ground steadily in the weeks that followed, mostly because no further attacks occurred. Since the economy could return to normal, the stock market did as well. On September 11, however, it was not obvious that such a rapid return to normalcy could be achieved. That good news was signaled by the *absence* of more bad news, and the market celebrated. The 20 percent increase in the S&P 500 that followed the steep drop after the terrible event was not a bubble.

While the market as a whole has not plummeted and stayed there, shares of wide classes of firms, such as the dot-com companies, have. The pattern conforms to the predictions of the best bubble theories. Bubblelike behavior should be more common for firms with highly ambiguous prospects, firms engulfed in Knightian uncertainty. Firms like Amazon.com that are prospecting in new territory. But such firms are not the majority. In contrast, old-economy stocks—which do make up the majority—are fairly well understood, and their price movements may comfortably match the predictions of the free-market theologians. During the two years that were dominated by the collapse of high-tech shares, for example, the old-economy "36er" stocks identified by my coauthor, James Glassman, and myself in *Dow 36,000* continued their climb upward, outperforming the tech-influenced S&P 500 by almost 30 percent.

Some firms are more prone to the bubble malady than others. By using the notion of ambiguity, it is relatively easy to identify suspects. A bubble can be detected by comparing the behavior of firms at the frontier and those far from it—just as the effects of a medicine on a particular disease can be discerned by comparing the clinical response of patients receiving the medication with the experience of those receiving a placebo. If all firms decline and there is no clear news—as was the case in the 1987 crash—strong conclusions are elusive. If some firms increase sharply for no apparent reason while other firms barely budge, a bubble may be forming.

A prudent and cautious investor, considering the purchase of shares in firms involved in a new and highly ambiguous (but potentially rewarding) activity, can pursue a bubble-wary investment strategy by taking a few easy steps. First, construct a watch list that includes the firms of interest. Gather a list of comparison stocks: dusty old firms with well-understood businesses and long track records. The Dow Jones Industrial Average is just such a list. Keep track of the news stories arriving each day and their impact on the share prices of the two sets of firms. If shares on the watch list appear to post enormous price changes relative to the movements in the overall market for mysterious reasons—on days without news— alarms should go off. This is especially true if the Dow companies are not doing so. An investor should be wary of purchasing the stocks that may be increasing in price for no good reason. The possibility that a bubble is forming is real.

That strategy has much to recommend it. Unexpected news, after all, is the source of fluctuation when the market is working well; movement on little news signals that the market may not be functioning properly. The strategy is easy to follow in the Internet age. Any investor with access to an online financial service can set up a personal portfolio. The service then constantly updates the price of each firm in an individual's portfolio and informs the client of any important news stories as well. If firms in the bubble-suspect group see their share price fluctuate more often when there is little or no news than the control firms' prices do, anyone willing to devote a few minutes a day to scan their watch list can detect the pattern.

The strategy makes sense and is easy to follow. But is it worth trying?

THE ANATOMY OF A BUBBLE

Of all the ridiculous booms and busts in the twentieth century, the astonishing advance of dot-coms and their subsequent collapse was the champion. Companies with at best skimpy prospects became billion-dollar success stories overnight. Celebrities lobbied high-tech venture capitalists to be put on their friends-and-family lists and be first in line when shares were initially issued to the public. Seasoned observers, even those bullish about stocks in general, unanimously warned of disaster. And disaster came.

With such a story line, it should be easy to declare the dot-com experience a bubble and move on, but if we want to learn something beyond what is now the conventional wisdom, then we have to dig deeper and not rely on anecdotes. What hard evidence is there that the Internet was a bubble? Practically none. The few researchers who have worked extensively on the issue, including Robert Hall in his famous Ely lecture, have found the opposite: Prices of some of the Internet firms might have been justified.

But in the context of the work described in this book, that answer hardly seems satisfactory. Bubbles are logically possible, and the Internet seemed the most promising example. It involved a new technology at the frontier of our understanding, where ambiguity was highest. The Internet would obviously change everyone's life, but nobody knew exactly how, or which firms would profit the most from the new world order. News accounts vividly described waves of stock buying as promising tidbits were passed from one person to the next. It is remarkable how precisely the circumstances of the Internet experience conform to the predictions of the bubble theories. Relying on the lessons of the past few chapters, it is time to take a second look.

HOW IT ALL STARTED

To many researchers the seeds of the Internet boom were planted in the early 1980s, when many people acquired enormous fortunes because of the success of the first generation of computer pioneers.

In 1975 Harvard dropout Bill Gates and his friend Paul Allen decided to commercialize their pet project, Basic, a new computer language that allowed hobbyists to write their own programs on the Altair 8800. Six years later, the two computer enthusiasts got their big break. To compete with Apple and the other makers of personal computers, IBM was rolling out one of its own. The computer giant asked Allen and Gates to commercialize the operating system DOS for that computer. Soon IBM-compatible PCs running on DOS—warts and all—captured the PC market. By the mid-1980s, Microsoft's Windows made the personal computer accessible to everyone. Gates and Allen became cultural icons.

Fame was not the only reward. The amount of cash generated by their success was astonishing. In 1986, Microsoft sold its first shares of stock to the public. Demand was strong for the hot new technology stock— the price of the initial offering was a surprisingly high $21. By early 1999, the success of Microsoft had pushed the share price to unfathomable heights. An investor who purchased $5,000 of Microsoft stock on that first day of trading was sitting on a stake worth $2 million. Even small investors benefited from that surge. Chief among them were Microsoft employees, who received stock options as part of their compensation package. Hundreds or even thousands of them became millionaires.

Microsoft's story was not an isolated case. Savvy investors who perceived the long-run potential of the personal computer in the 1980s had a hard time picking losers. A shareholder who put $5,000 into Dell shares in the late 1980s saw that stake climb to $3 million by 1999. Investors in Intel, the maker of microchips that powered the PCs, saw their stake increase by a factor of one hundred in little more than a decade. Shareholders of Compaq and Applied Materials were equally happy. The lesson that many learned was this: Recognize a new technology wave early and become a millionaire.

Then came another new wave. The conceptual foundation of the Internet dates to the early 1960s, when MIT scientist Leonard Kleinrock published a theoretical paper that described how computers might communicate over a network by trading packets of information. In the 1960s,

the Department of Defense had recognized the potential
strategic importance of Kleinrock's vision—a major inter-
linked computer network—and allocated funds to construct the ARPANET, a network named after the Defense
Advanced Research Projects Agency. The Internet remained a technical backwater inhabited by geeks and
nerds until 1991, when Mark MaCahill of the University
of Minnesota distributed his Internet search program,
named Gopher. Suddenly individuals could sift through
the many sites linked to the Internet and extract the information that they sought. In 1995, companies such as
America Online (AOL) began offering households access
to the Internet.

By 1999, the Internet had clearly demonstrated its
revolutionary economic force. Business was moving rapidly to the Web, and new forms of electronically based
commerce emerged that had been figments of the imagi-
nation. Amazon.com allowed individuals for the first time
to browse through a bookstore that offered almost every
book in print and delivered purchases the next day. eBay
combined America's garage sales and linked them to soft-
ware that managed sophisticated auctions.

Like the Microsoft millionaires before them, those
who noticed the economic potential of the Internet early
were rewarded handsomely. People who invested $5,000
in Amazon.com at its initial public offering saw the value
of their holding grow to $140,000 in less than two years.
The same stake in eBay, which first sold shares on
September 23, 1998, was worth almost $83,000 a little
more than one year later. But those healthy sums were
minor compared with what was to come.

You can't start a gold rush without gold. By early
1999, easy money was everywhere, and panicked buying

of shares occurred. Any company even remotely connected to the Internet saw its share price increase, often tenfold. Amid the chaos, two distinct phenomena emerged. First, prices for first-tier firms—which plausibly were good business—soared even higher. The value of that $5,000 stake in Amazon.com grew to almost $300,000, while eBay shares tripled. Second, a blizzard of new offerings with extraordinarily shaky prospects hit the floor of the stock exchange, and investors gobbled up those shares as well.

Typical of the latter group was theglobe.com. The Web service, which began as an agglomeration of community homepages with highly questionable potential for revenue, had a target price set by its investment banker of $9 per share. To many, that price, which gave the firm a total market valuation of well over $100 million, seemed absurd. How could theglobe.com possibly earn enough profit to justify the valuation? Such concerns seemed misplaced at the public offering on November 12, 1998. Demand was so high that the firm's shares jumped on their first day of trading to $97 per share, which made the entire firm worth close to $1 billion. Those concerns do resonate more now. Like many of its peers whose values reached similar heights, theglobe.com failed miserably. In August 2001, the firm stopped operating its webpage, and its stock sold on the Over-the-Counter bulletin board for a measly 7 cents a share.

That episode exhibits almost paradoxical contradictions. Businesses without apparent hope of long-run profitability skyrocketed. Pundits unanimously diagnosed the insanity, and share prices eventually complied by returning to earth with a loud thud. At the same time, the craze was built on a solid foundation. We can draw sensible lessons from the first wave of experience with computer technology and hard profits in the pockets of high-tech investors.

A SIMPLE TEST

But was the dot-com experience a bubble? The circumstances are certainly suspicious. Those firms might have taken over the world, but the probabilities associated with that outcome were unknowable. The price rose and dropped in a classic bubble pattern. The key question was whether any information could have signaled trouble. Could the watch-list strategy outlined above have saved an investor money?

I investigated how an investor might have fared if he had followed the watch-list strategy in early 1999, before the prices for many Internet firms soared and collapsed. I collected data for firms listed on the Dow Jones Composite Internet Index and on the Hambrecht and Quist Group Internet Index. (The full list of these firms is contained in the appendix in the back of this book.) Firms included in the Dow Jones Industrial Average were the control group. I then performed the following experiment: I selected the five biggest movements for each individual stock during the bubble period and thoroughly searched news accounts on those days. The bubble question then became simple. Did the Internet firms tend to move more on days of little or no news?

The definition of *news* is, of course, difficult to pin down. To sidestep arbitrary decisions about the newsworthiness of particular events, I sorted all the stories into six piles that divided the movements by the quality of the news that caused it. The items in the first few piles clearly reported material events that could have a large effect on the long-run prospects of firms, while the higher-numbered piles contained news stories of more questionable relevance.

Specifically, an event was categorized as a 1 if a large price swing coincided with that firm's announcement or preannouncement of earnings. A typical 1 was the 9 percent increase in share prices for Sears stock that occurred after the company announced skyrocketing same-store sales growth and higher-than-expected earnings on April 5, 2000. Category 2 included major mergers and acquisitions, lawsuits, or fundamental reorganizations of a firm or industry. Typical of these was the 1998 news that the merger between Exxon and Mobil might be challenged by the government. This was important news for Dow component Chevron, a key competitor, and its share price jumped sharply in response. Category 3 included news events that mentioned the remarks or coverage changes of analysts. On June 23, 2000, for example, Morgan Stanley Dean Witter analyst Mary Meeker said that Amazon would not meet her revenue targets. Amazon share prices plunged. Category 4 events were announcements of new contracts or strategic alliances with other firms. Sometimes these are clearly great news about a firm's potential future success, and sometimes it is hard to tell. On March 1, 1995, for example, AOL announced that it had entered a joint venture agreement with Bertelsmann to offer online service in Europe. AOL share prices increased sharply because of the promise of many new customers. Category 5 included published interviews with corporate insiders or other news stories and new-product announcements. On May 23, 1995, for example, network equipment manufacturer Cisco Systems introduced a new product that reduced the cost and complexity of operating networks. The company's price increased in response. An event was categorized as a 6 if no identifiable news occurred on the days surrounding the big movement. On November 3, 1995, health service provider Cybercare experienced just such a move, increasing 25 percent for no apparent reason.

For each firm, the news category numbers were averaged to create an information score. A firm with a 1 would have posted its biggest price changes on days with announcements about earnings. A firm with a 6 would have moved only on days with absolutely no news.

If there were a bubble, one would expect to see a large fraction of the movements in share price concentrated in the higher-numbered categories, especially category 6, where there is no news at all. If most major movements coincided with earnings announcements or lower numbers, a bubble likely did not occur.

The results of the exercise clearly indicate something strange in the late 1990s with the Internet firms. First, take a look at the Dow companies. Fully 55 percent of them saw their share prices move on average with category 1 or category 2 news events. A high percentage of the major share price movements occurred on days with highly relevant news about the firm. The pattern is exactly what we should expect in a well-functioning market. The rest of the major movements occurred with slightly less tangible news—category 3. None of the firms, on average, experienced frequent major price swings on days with weak or no news.

The Internet firms were much different. None posted a large movement on a day of earnings news! Almost 60 percent of them moved on days with the three lowest categories of news. Eight percent tended to move on days with no news. Typical of these was the firm Infospace, which provided infrastructure services on multiple computer platforms. The shares of this firm fluctuated wildly for no apparent reason. The distribution is the opposite for the old-economy Dow firms—and a strong signal that the market was behaving oddly. The pattern is exactly what we would expect with a bubble. Share prices were moving for unidentifiable reasons, and the simple bubble-scope would have sounded a loud alarm.

AMBIGUITY AND RISK

Other indicators of market inefficiencies have not stood up well to evaluation. A bubble indication becomes a smoking gun only if we can prove that it could have been used in real time to detect important warning signals. The P/E model that figured so prominently in recent popular bubble literature has failed that simple test. A real-world test of the model showed that relying on it would have been a very bad investment strategy.

How should ambiguity affect markets? If the market is functioning well, the return to the shareholder should compensate for the greater ambiguity. Firms that tend to move on little or no news are riskier and should pay a premium to shareholders. Conversely, if a bubble exists, we should see the opposite pattern. Firms with prices soaring for no apparent reason should subsequently see those prices collapse since the increase was not justified by fundamentals in the first place. The few Internet firms that respond primarily to news might have escaped the bubble and been solid investments.

What if you had invested only in those Internet firms that moved on tangible information and had avoided firms that moved on nothing at all? To assess which pattern held during the Internet boom, I used information scores to break the universe of Internet firms up into different portfolios. For a fair test, the portfolios were classified by information type based on their largest movements before January 1999, a period that preceded the most striking collapses in prices. The same portfolios were constructed for the Dow companies. The rate of return for each information category between January 1999 and May 2001— a month well past the pop—was calculated for firms in each information group.

The results are striking. For the Dow companies, we see exactly the pattern that would be expected by efficient-market gurus if this new measure of ambiguity provides additional information about risk. As ambiguity increases, the market views firms as riskier, and their expected return rises to compensate. Firms with an information score of 1 averaged a 7.5 percent decrease in price between January 1999 and May 2001. Firms with a score of 2 increased 18.5 percent; with a score of 3, 20 percent. If you invested in the Dow companies moving on little news, you were taking a big chance, and you received a healthy reward for that daring.

The Internet firms exhibited the opposite pattern. Firms with an average information score of 2 returned 137 percent over that period: The group consisted mainly of blue-chip Internet firms such as Novell, Sun Microsystems, and Microsoft. Firms with a score of 3, a group that included AOL and Cisco, also had healthy returns, increasing 75 percent. Firms in the higher categories had far less rosy experiences, with category 5 and 6 firms dropping significantly over the period. On average, an investment in firms that had been soaring on no news made no money. Typical of their experience was OpenMarket, whose share price dropped from a high of almost $66 to about $1.50 in May 2001.

The simple exercise with news identified the winners and the losers in the Internet horserace well before the dot-com crash. An investment in Internet firms that had previously increased in response to tangible news *more than doubled* during the suspect period. If you invested $10,000 in firms with an information score of 2 in 1999, that stake turned into $23,700 by May 2001. The results confirm that the watch-list strategy is sound.

A BUBBLE EXPOSED

A bubble appears to have been captured. Prices swung wildly on little or no news. Identifying firms in the Internet sector furthest from the craziness proved a profitable investment strategy. But the bubble was not as fierce a beast as might have been expected from listening to news accounts. Most important, the few good Internet firms that increased on solid news returned so much that an equal investment in each firm listed on the two Internet indexes made money between January 1999 and May 2001. A stake in all Internet firms increased by a healthy 41 percent over that two-year period. If you invested $10,000 in every Internet firm at the start of

1999 and held strong while the bubble burst, you would have earned $4,100.

Such high profits during the bubble period are surprising, but the distribution of the profits suggests why news stories focused on the collapse. About half the Internet firms in those indexes increased in price over the entire bubble period, and about half decreased in price, with many drops approaching 100 percent. The half that declined sharply figured more prominently in news accounts, which tend to focus on the negative.

The popular perception of the Internet experience may be quite different from those results for one other reason. The experiment involved investing in firms that existed in January 1999. Many of the worst horror stories during the Internet debacle involved stocks first offered for sale to the public after that date. The distinction is striking. An alternative investment strategy that purchased newly issued shares beginning in 1999 and held them through May 2001 would have been disastrous, with a return of minus 62 percent. Almost every new issue during the bubble period was junk. Typical of that group was eToys, the online toy store that burned through hundreds of millions of dollars and is now bankrupt. Of the twenty-eight new firms that made it onto our two indexes, only one—Juniper Networks—increased significantly after its first public offering, while twenty-one posted returns relative to their initial price of minus 70 percent or more!

Historians will immediately recognize the similarity between that episode and other purported bubbles. When prices are soaring and buying is frenzied, unscrupulous merchants take advantage of the unwary. That pattern was apparent even in the Dutch Tulipmania. In responding to

Peter Garber's claim that Tulipmania was *not* a mania, MIT economist Charles Kindleberger once wrote that "Garber acknowledges that he cannot explain why garden variety tulips like the Gouda, Switzer or White Frown, traded among simple folk at so-called 'colleges' or public houses, also soared and fell in price." In our time, the big investment houses sold shares of dubious quality to equally unsuspecting investors.

The existence of those patterns is at odds with the view that an investor can blindly trust the market to deliver a fair price for any asset. An investor needs to be watchful. The returns to that systematic watchfulness are significant. The history of the dot-com bubble provides an invaluable indication of what to look for.

But the constant give-and-take between those who believe in bubbles and those who do not suggests an important caution. If the approach outlined in this chapter withstands counterattack, then it may be incorporated into the mechanism that the market uses to set the price of stocks in the future. At that point, an investment strategy based upon the avoidance of firms that have large price movements on shaky news will not outperform the market. If this occurs, however, the type of bubbles discussed in the literature will most likely become extinct. Whenever share prices surge for no good reason, investors will recognize the warning signs and sell.

Which suggests two possibilities. The first is that nothing changes, in which case the follow-the-news strategy may again be quite profitable in the future, as it was in the past. Since Knightian uncertainty may be an indelible part of life, this scenario is quite plausible. The second is that the market adjusts, in which case it will be more difficult for a bubble to form because a new safety valve has been introduced. It pays the investor, however, to monitor the market carefully *in either case*. If the worst happens, new-economy shares of some type will emerge in the future, and their swings will occur only in response to hard news. It will then be easy to accomplish something that was impossible during the Internet craze: owning the shares and sleeping at night, too.

CHAPTER NINE

Conclusion

[The Shareholder and the Philosopher are walking down a flight of stairs. At the bottom is a door with a sign that reads "Ergodicity Room"]

PHILOSOPHER: *We have almost finished the tour of my laboratory. There is one more room you must see; it's my favorite project.*

SHAREHOLDER: *That sign has a word that I have never seen before. How do you say it?*

PHILOSOPHER: *Er-god-icity. Say it as if it has god in the middle.*

SHAREHOLDER: *What does it mean?*

PHILOSOPHER: *It just might be the most important word in the English language. Before I explain it, tell me: How do you physically observe the financial world?*

SHAREHOLDER: *I gather facts and data concerning the things I am interested in and analyze them.*

PHILOSOPHER: *Where do those facts come from?*

SHAREHOLDER: *I rely on many sources—newspapers, television, and so on.*

PHILOSOPHER: *That's not what I mean. Where do the facts and data come from? What generates them?*

SHAREHOLDER: *I never quite thought of it that way before, but I suppose that since I am studying these facts and data and looking for patterns that provide useful investment advice, I implicitly am assuming that there is—beneath it all—some ultimately knowable process that generates all the data.*

PHILOSOPHER: *Exactly. The laws of gravity were a great example of that. Newton's theories explained a number of previously puzzling observations. After the laws of gravity were understood, phenomena that had been a mystery made perfect sense. Why? The data on planetary motions had, if you like, been produced by a data-generating process that was previously unknown. Until Newton's discovery, the search for that process was physics. The progress we have made is miraculous. After all, Newton never would have found the laws if he did not believe they existed before he began his search! What drove him to believe that?*

SHAREHOLDER: *What does all this have to do with ergodicity?*

PHILOSOPHER: *Like the data on the movement of planets, the data we analyze from financial markets is the result of some underlying data-generating process. If that process, no matter how complex, is the same over time, then repeated observation and analysis will ultimately reveal it to us. If that process is constantly changing, however, then research may just spin us in circles. Just when we think we have the data-generating process nailed, it changes. If research is to be truly informative, the data-generating process must be ergodic—changeless through time. Newton was sure before he started that such immutable laws existed. For financial phenomena, it's not nearly as obvious that they always do.*

SHAREHOLDER: *And that's what you look for in this room.*

PHILOSOPHER: *Quite so. And we have made great progress. Surprisingly, many aspects of our financial world appear ergodic. There really are laws of finance that are nearly as immutable as those of gravity. But for bubble research, the question is especially complicated. Since bubbles appear to arise when experience is the weakest, the entire notion of ergodicity might not apply. If bubbles reside where things are new, then they are only the same over time if there is something unchanging and predictable about the way that new things form.*

SHAREHOLDER: *Is there?*

PHILOSOPHER: *We don't know yet, but there are only two possibilities. The first is that there are such rules that govern the expansion of the frontier of our economic universe. Once these are discovered, bubbles will likely cease to exist. The ambiguous breeding ground for bubbles will be too well understood to allow their creation. The second possibility is that each new thing appears like a spark from the heavens with no apparent relationship to the new thing that preceded it. Knowledge of the entire history of the frontier provides almost no guidance concerning what will happen next. If that turns out to be the truth about our world, bubbles will likely stay with us forever.*

SHAREHOLDER: *I hope the latter is the truth. This world would be a very boring place if we understood it perfectly.*

PHILOSOPHER: *That's why the latter probably is the truth.*

On January 24, 1848, a California construction superintendent named James Marshall discovered gold while he was building a sawmill on the South Fork of the American River. Word spread rapidly that gold had been found on the mill property owned by John Sutter, and men immediately swarmed the rivers of California prospecting with shovels and pocketknives. For the first men, there was much gold to be found. Lucky prospector Job Dye and a "gang of Indians" collected 273 pounds of gold in just seven weeks. Miners along the American River had average daily earnings ranging from $800 to $15,000. News of these events spread gold fever across America.

California was practically empty when gold was first discovered, but news of gold caused a migration of unprecedented scale to occur. Vagabonds were not the only participants in that migration. Men from every corner of America left their families behind and headed to the goldfields. One prospector described his (rather typical) party as consisting of "two ministers and two doctors, as well as blacksmiths, carpenters, tailors, shoemakers and many other mechanics." By the end of the rush, five hundred thousand immigrants called California their home.

Even after the first wave, many found the gold they were looking for. One sign of the unbelievable success of the miners was the sharp increase in the price of everything else. A boiled egg cost 75 cents. A $2,000 steam engine sold for $15,000. One busy prostitute earned $50,000 in 1849 alone, while a farmer earned $25,000 selling his vegetables. Rents in San Francisco, the nearest population center, soared, with a canvas tent near a hotel in that town renting for $40,000 a year.

But, of course, many found disappointment. They left their families and loved ones behind, and returned years later with nothing to show for their efforts.

One hundred fifty years later, the Internet boom set off a similar type of gold rush with many telling parallels. While some of the earliest prospectors became rich beyond their wildest dreams (and paid a fortune for San

Francisco real estate), many ordinary investors lost significant portions of their hard-earned savings by investing
in shaky companies whose prices were inflated for no
good reason. But the problem facing these investors was
as difficult as that facing would-be forty-niners. New territory, previously unexplored, appeared to be littered with
gold. Nobody could be sure how much gold was hidden
there; but if gold was there, then the early birds would be
the fattest.

Both of these episodes fit neatly into the view of bubbles that has survived the give-and-take between the warring conventional wisdoms. Bubbles exist, but they are
not everywhere. They emerge where the economic world
is the newest, where information is the poorest. They happen when the opportunity for great profit is real, but they
are shrouded in ambiguity. Another such episode will
almost certainly occur.

So when the next rush occurs, we will each have to
decide once again whether to participate. Should *you* purchase the wildest high-tech stocks again? History provides clues about how to make that decision prudently.
First, stay away from firms that increase in price sharply
when there is no news. The best firms will make money
and increase in price when the market learns that they will
make even more money. Second, when the frenzy is at its
highest, unwary shareholders gobble up everything that
Wall Street is willing to throw their way. Wall Street has
never ignored a chance to make a quick profit, and,
accordingly, new offerings appear in unusually good times
that have unusually bleak prospects. Don't buy them!

When the gold rush occurred, California was a vacant
backwater. The state had no banks, roads, and factories,
and almost no citizens. Farmers and ranchers were about

the only folks who could earn a living. As prospectors built roads to the mines, towns grew up at their intersections. Rivers that provided little gold proved to be tremendously valuable tools of commerce. Skilled craftsmen who abandoned the East Coast in a failed search for gold set up shop and prospered anyway. Similarly, the Internet boom stimulated investment spending that has profoundly reshaped and improved our lives.

So bubbles can happen, but they often accompany wonderful discoveries. Will it happen again? While some may believe that the days of the frontier are behind us, the opposite is most likely true. According to Stanford economist Paul Romer, the information-technology revolution enhances our ability to try new ideas and explore new possibilities. New economic frontiers will emerge with increasing frequency as a result. This is both scary and exhilarating. A unique willingness to push the frontier perhaps explains better than anything else the remarkable success of the American economy. Yet that wealth has come in uneven spurts, with many false starts. Fortunes were made, and fortunes were lost.

In the end, however, those who decided to stay on the farm in upstate New York and skip the gold rush did not acquire great wealth. Some of those who marched off to California did. And both were better off because so many were willing to risk it all and head for the frontier.

Notes

Preface

PAGE

15 Kaletsky, Anatol. "Beware the Net Bubble," *The Times* (London), December 16, 1998.

15 Mackay, Charles. *Extraordinary Popular Delusions and the Madness of Crowds.* Boston: L.C. Page and Company, 1932.

1. Bubbles, Markets, and Frontiers

23 Hayek, Friedrich A. *The Road to Serfdom.* Chicago: The University of Chicago Press, 1944.

26 Wooley, Leonard C. *The Sumerians.* Oxford: The Clarendon Press, 1928.

28 Knight, Frank. *Risk, Uncertainty, and Profit.* Boston and New York: Houghton Mifflin Company, 1921.

30 Ellsberg, Daniel. Thesis, "Risk, Ambiguity, and Decision," 1963, Harvard University, Cambridge, Mass.

32 *New York Times.* "'Casino Mentality' Linked to Day Trading Stresses," August 1, 1999.

34 *The Economist.* "Predicting the Unpredictable," May 31, 2001.

34 *New York Times.* "Declaration of Independence Found in a $4 Picture Frame," April 3, 1991.

36 Huberman, Gur, and Regev, Tomer. "Contagious Speculation and a Cure for Cancer: A Nonevent that Made Stock Prices Soar," *The Journal of Finance*, 2001, vol. 56, no. 1: 387–96.

38 de la Vega, Josef. *Confusion de Confusiones*, S-Gravenhage, M. Nijhoff, 1939.

2. The Price Is Right!

41 Malkiel, Burton. *A Random Walk Down Wall Street.* New York: Norton 1973.

42 Hazlett, Thomas W. "Hayek's Heroes," *Reason,* December 1999.

44 Friedman, Milton. *Essays in Positive Economics.* Chicago: University of Chicago Press, 1966.

51 Hall, Robert E. The Richard T. Ely Lecture, "Struggling to Understand the Stock Market," May 2001, AEA Papers and Proceedings.

3. Rational Leaps of Faith

57 Bachelier, Louis. *"Theorie de la Speculation" Annales de l'Ecole normale superiure* (trans. *Random Character of Stock Market Prices*), 1900. Peter Bernstein is the modern scholar normally credited with the discovery of Bachelier's work.

58 Kendall, Maurice. "The Analysis of Economic Time Series—Part 1: Prices," *Journal of the Royal Statistical Society*, 1953, vol. 96: 11–25.

58 Samuelson, Paul. "Proof that Properly Anticipated Prices Fluctuate Properly," *Industrial Management Review*, Spring 1965: 41–49.

61 Fama, Eugene F. "Efficient Capital Markets: A Review of Theory and Empirical Work," *The Journal of Finance*, 1970, vol. 31, no. 1: 383–417.

61 ———, "Efficient Capital Markets: II," *The Journal of Finance,* 1991, vol. 46, no. 5.

62 Rubinstein, Mark. "Rational Markets: Yes or No? The Affirmative Case," *Financial Analysts Journal*, May–June 2001. This is by far the most readable and best-thought-out defense of efficient-market theory in recent years. Rubinstein's brilliant analysis is drawn on throughout the book.

63 Fama, Eugene F. "Efficient Capital Markets: A Review of Theory and Empirical Work," *The Journal of Finance*, 1970, vol. 31, no. 1: 383–417.

63 ———, "Efficient Capital Markets: II," *The Journal of Finance,* 1991, vol. 46, no. 5.

65 Scholes, Myron. "The Market for Securities: Substitution versus Price Pressure and Effects of Information on Share Prices," *Journal of Business*, 1972, vol. 45: 179–211.

66 Jensen, Michael. "Some Anomalous Evidence Regarding Economic Efficiency," *Journal of Financial Economics,* 1978, vol. 6: 95–101.

4. Bubbles Everywhere?

69 Keynes, John Maynard. *The General Theory of Employment, Interest, and Money.* London: Macmillan and Co., 1936.

71 Cass, David, and Shell, Karl. "Do Sunspots Matter?" *Journal of Political Economy*, 1978, vol. 91, no. 21: 193–227.

71 Jevons' sunspot work was first published in a volume he edited, *Investigations in Currency and Finance.* London: Foxwell, 1884.

74 Blanchard, Olivier, and Watson, Mark. "Bubbles, Rational Expectations and Financial Markets," *Crises in the Economic and Financial Structure,* P. Wachtel, ed. Lexington, Mass.: D.C. Heath and Company, 1982. This is also available at the NBER website www.nber.org.

75 Shiller, Robert. "Do Stock Prices Move Too Much to Be Justified by Subsequent Changes in Dividends?" *American Economic Review*, 1981, vol. 71: 421–36.

75 LeRoy, Stephen, and Porter, Richard. "The Present Value Relation: Tests Based on Variance Bounds," *Econometrica*, 1981, vol. 49: 555–77.

78 Marsh, T. A. and Merton, R. "Dividend Variability and Variance Bounds Tests for the Rationality of Stock Market Prices," *American Economic Review*, 1986, vol. 76: 483–98.

80 Krugman, Paul. "Reckonings: A Leap in the Dark," *New York Times,* January 5, 2000.

5. The Farmboy and the Fugitive

85 Knight, Frank. *Risk, Uncertainty, and Profit.* Boston, New York: Houghton Mifflin Company, 1921.

88 Keynes, John Maynard. *Treatise on Probability.* London: Macmillan and Co., 1929.

89 Savage, Leonard. *The Foundations of Statistics.* New York: John Wiley & Sons, 1954.

90 Ellsberg, Daniel. "Risk, Ambiguity, and the Savage Axioms," *Quarterly Journal of Economics*, 1961, vol. 75: 643–69.

93 Gell-Mann, Murray. *The Quark and the Jaguar: Adventures in the Simple and the Complex.* New York: W. H. Freeman and Co., 1994.

96 For those wishing more detail than I offer on behavioral finance, Daniel Kahneman and Amos Tversky are the giants in the field of behavioral finance whose work has influenced all modern scholars. Their book, which is coauthored by Paul Slovic, titled *Judgment Under Uncertainty: Heuristics and Biases* (Cambridge University Press, 1982), contains many of their most important papers. Robert Shiller and Andrei Shleifer are two of the leading economists who have advanced the field in recent years. Shleifer's highly readable book *Inefficient Markets: An Introduction to Behavioral Finance* (Oxford University Press, 2000) is a must read for any serious financial scholar, and Shiller's famed *Irrational Exuberance* (Princeton University Press, 2000) is a very well-written introduction to the field.

96 Becker, Selwyn, and Brownson, Fred. "What Price Ambiguity? Or the Role of Ambiguity in Decision-Making," *Journal of Political Economy*, 1964, vol. 72: 62–73.

96 MacCrimmon, Kenneth. "Descriptive and Normative Implications of the Decision-Theory Postulates," *Risk and Uncertainty: Proceedings of a Conference Held by the Internal Economic Association*, eds. Borch, Karl, and Mossin, Jan. London, Melbourne: Macmillan and Co.; New York: St. Martin's Press, 1968.

96 Hogarth, Robin, and Kunreuther, Howard. "Decision Making under Ignorance: Arguing with Yourself," *Journal of Risk and Uncertainty*, 1995, vol. 10: 15–36.

97 Slovic, Paul, and Tversky, Amos. "Who Accepts Savage's Axiom?" *Behavioral Science*, 1974, vol. 19: 368–73.

97 Asch, Solomon. *Social Psychology.* Englewood Cliffs, N.J.: Prentice Hall, 1952.

97 Asch, Solomon. "Studies of Independence and Conformity: A Minority of One Against a Unanimous Majority," *Psychological Monographs*, 1956, vol. 70, no. 416.

98 Bond, R., and Smith, P. "Culture and Conformity: A Meta-analysis of Studies Using Aschs (1952b, 1956) Line Judgement Task," *Psychological Bulletin*, 1996, vol. 118: 111–37.

99 Schmeidler, David. "Subjective Probability and Expected Utility Without Additivity," *Econometrica*, 1989, vol. 57, no. 3: 571–87.

99 Gilboa, Itzhak, and Schmeidler, David. "Maxmin Expected Utility With Non-Unique Prior," *Journal of Mathematical Economics*, 1989, vol. 18: 141–53.

102 For a further review of Knightian uncertainty, see Basili, Marcello, "Knightian Uncertainty in Financial Markets: An Assessment," February 2000, Università degli Studi di Siena, Dipartimento di Economia Politica, Siena, Italy.

6. Attack of the Killer Anomalies

107 Rubinstein, Mark. "Rational Markets: Yes or No? The Affirmative Case," *Financial Analysts Journal*, May–June 2001.

107 O'Higgins, Michael. *Beating the Dow: A High-Return, Low-Risk Method for Investing in the Dow Jones Industrial Stocks With as Little as 5,000.* New York: HarperCollins, 1991.

110 Rubinstein, Mark. "Rational Markets: Yes or No? The Affirmative Case," *Financial Analysts Journal*, May–June 2001.

112 DeBondt, Werner, and Thaler, Richard. "Further Evidence on Investor Overreaction and Stock Market Seasonality," *The Journal of Finance*, 1987, vol. 3: 557–81.

116 Shleifer, Andrei. *Inefficient Markets: An Introduction to Behavioral Science.* Oxford: Oxford University Press, 2000.

117 ———.

120 Shiller, Robert. "Speculative Prices and Popular Models," *Journal of Economic Perspectives*, 1990, vol. 4, no. 2: 55–65.

121 Cutler, David, Poterba, James, and Summers, Lawrence. "What Moves Stock Prices?" *Journal of Portfolio Management*, 1989, vol. 15, no. 3.

122 Johnson, Neil F., et al. "Application of Multi-Agent Games to the Prediction of Financial Time-Series," *Physica A*, 2001, vol. 299: 222–27.

122 Lamper, D., and Howison, S. "Predictability of Large Future Changes in a Competitive Evolving Population," *Physical Review*

Letters, vol. 88. See also Lamper's many other contributions at
www.maths.ox.ac.uk/~lamper/frameset.html.

7. Revenge of the Nerds

127 Garber, Peter. *Famous First Bubbles: The Fundamentals of Early Manias.* Cambridge, Mass.: The MIT Press, 2000. The fictionalized trip by our two gentleman to the flower shop is meant as a brief intuitive summary of part of Garber's argument, not as a historical document of the price of *Semper Augustus* bulbs many years later. There is no substitute for the reading of his marvelous book, which I encourage wholeheartedly.

130 Camerer, Colin F., Babcock, Linda, Loewenstein, George, and Thaler, Richard. "Labor Supply of New York City Cab Drivers: One Day at a Time," *The Quarterly Journal of Economics*, 112: 2, 407–41.

137 Glassman, James K., and Hassett, Kevin. *Dow 36,000: The New Strategy for Profiting from the Coming Rise in the Stock Market.* New York: Times Business, 1999.

137 Smith, Mark. *Toward Rational Exuberance.* New York: Farrar, Straus and Giroux, 2001.

138 Siegel, Jeremy. *Stocks for the Long Run: A Guide to Selecting Markets for Long-Term Growth.* Burr Ridge, Ill: Irwin, 1994.

138 Jorion, Philippe, and Goetzmann, William. "Global Stock Markets in the Twentieth Century," *The Journal of Finance*, 1999, vol. 54, no. 3: 953–80.

8. Bubblespotting

147 The "36er" stocks we identified are Automatic Data Processing; Campbell Soup Company; Cintas Corporation; Cisco Systems, Inc; Coca-Cola Co.; DeVRY, Inc.; Fannie Mae, General Electric Company; Gillette Company; Johnson & Johnson; Landauer, Inc.; Microsoft Corporation; RPM Incorporated; Tootsie Roll Industries; and Wells Fargo & Co. The average rate of return was 8.05 percent from September 1, 1999 to December 31, 2001. Standard and Poor's 500 (without dividends) average return was −13.75 percent, and the Nasdaq Composite (without dividends) was −29.10 percent.

154 For a complete list of companies, see the Appendix, where companies are presented according to their information category vari-

able. The news events were categorized by Ken Fears, and the data are available upon request. The categorization process involved a number of judgments. The most important was the treatment of moves that appeared to be in the wrong direction relative to the news. If an earnings announcement appeared, relative to consensus, to be a positive surprise, but the share price declined, then one might wish to call that a move unrelated to news, since the share price moved in the opposite of the expected direction. We chose instead to classify moves according to news event regardless of the direction of the move. Our reasoning was that the expectation of the market is unobservable, and the deviation of the news from the market's expectation the true objective.

154 *National Public Radio.* "Nightly Business Report," April 5, 2000.

154 AFX News. "Exxon/Mobil Proposed Link Reportedly Faces Probe by EU/US Regulators," November 27, 1998.

154 *CNNfn.* "Chernoff on the Nasdaq's Decline/Rhonda's Roundtable," June 23, 2000.

154 *PR Newswire.* "Bertelsmann, Ag and America Online, Inc. Announce European Joint Venture," March 1, 1995.

154 *Network World.* "Cisco to Roll Out New Token-Ring Routing Hub," May 2, 1995.

161 Kindleberger, Charles. *Maniacs, Panics, and Crashes—A History of Financial Crises.* New York: John Wiley & Sons, 1978.

9. Conclusion

165 Caughey, John W. *The California Gold Rush.* Berkeley: University of California Press, 1948.

166 Holliday, J. S. *The World Rushed In: The California Gold Rush Experience.* New York: Simon and Schuster, 1981.

Appendix

INTERNET FIRMS BY INFORMATION CATEGORY

NAME	TICKER
TYPE 2 INFORMATION	
Ameritrade Holding Corporation	AMTD
Microsoft Corporation	MSFT
Mindspring Enterprises Inc.	ELNK
Novell Inc.	NOVL
Qualcomm Inc.	QCOM
Sun Microsystems Inc.	SUNW
Verity Inc.	VRTY
TYPE 3 INFORMATION	
America Online Inc.	AOL
B E A Systems Inc.	BEAS
Checkfree Holdings Corporation	CKFR
Cisco Systems Inc.	CSCO
CNET Inc.	CNET
Cyber Care Inc.	CYBR

Cylink Corporation	CYLK
E Trade Group Inc.	ET
Level 3 Communications Inc.	LVLT
Macromedia Inc.	MACR
Psinet Inc.	PSIX
Qwest Communications Intl Inc.	Q
Secure Computing Corporation	SCUR
Sportsline.com Inc.	SPLN
3Com Corporation	COMS

TYPE 4 INFORMATION

Amazon.com Inc.	AMZN
At Home Corporation	ATHM
Broadcom Corporation	BRCM
Citrix Systems Inc.	CTXS
CMGI Inc.	CMGI
Convera (formerly Excaliber Tech. & Intel)	CNVR
Cybercash Inc.	CYCH
Doubleclick Inc.	DCLK
Egghead.com Inc.	EGGS
Infonautics Inc.	INFO
Intuit Inc.	INTU
LYCOS (now TERRA-LYCOS)	LCOS
Networks Associates Inc.	NETA
Open Market Inc.	OMKT
Realnetworks Inc.	RNWK
R S A Sec Inc.	RSAS
12 Technologies Inc.	ITWO
Verisign Inc.	VRSN
Yahoo Inc.	YHOO

TYPE 5 INFORMATION

Digital River Inc.	DRIV
eBay Inc.	EBAY
Exodus Communications Inc.	EXDS
Inktomi Corporation	INKT

Net Cruise	NETCE
Peapod Inc.	PPOD

TYPE 6 INFORMATION

Broadvision Inc.	BVSN
Infospace.com	INSP
Ticketmaster Inc.	TMCS
Voxware Inc.	VOXW

DOW INDUSTRIAL COMPANIES (1977) BY INFORMATION CATEGORY

NAME	TICKER

TYPE 1 INFORMATION

Bethlehem Steel Corporation	BS
Eastman Kodak Company	EK
Minnesota Mining & Manufacturing Company	MMM

TYPE 2 INFORMATION

Alcoa Inc.	AA
A T & T Corporation	T
Chevron Corporation	CHV
Du Pont E I De Nemours & Co.	DD
Exxon Mobil Corporation	XOM
Goodyear Tire & Rubber Company	GT
Procter & Gamble Company	PG
Texaco Inc.	TX
United Technologies Corporation	UTX

TYPE 3 INFORMATION

Fortune Brands Inc.	FO
General Electric Company	GE
General Motors Corporation	GM
Honeywell International Inc.	HON
Inco Ltd.	N
International Paper Company	IP
Johns Manville Corporation	JM

Sears Roebuck & Company	S
Union Carbide Corporation	UK
U S X Marathon Group	MRO

IPO'D AFTER JANUARY 1, 1999

NAME	TICKER
Akamai Technologies Inc.	AKAM
Ariba Inc.	ARBA
Chemdex Corporation	VNTR
Commerce One Inc.	CMRC
Covad Communications Group Inc.	COVD.OB
Critical Path Inc.	CPTH
Digital Island Inc.	ISLD
eToys Inc.	ETYS
HEALTHEON CORP	HLTH
Internet Capital Group Inc.	ICGE
Juniper Networks Inc.	JNPR
MP3.com Inc.	MPPP
Net2Phone Inc.	NTOP
Palm Inc.	PALM
Portal Software Inc.	PRSF
Priceline.com Inc.	PCLN
Promotions.com Inc.	PRMO
Red Hat Inc.	RHAT
Rhythms Netconnections Inc.	RTHM
Scient Corporation	SCNT
Starmedia Network Inc.	STRM
Sycamore Networks Inc.	SCMR
TIBCO Software Inc.	TIBX
Travelocity.com Inc.	TVLY
VerticalNet Inc.	VERT
Vignette Corporation	VIGN
Webmethods Inc.	WEBM
Webvan Group Inc.	WBVN

Acknowledgments

This book would not have been possible without the help and encouragement of many friends and colleagues. Jim Glassman got me started on the project, and helped me through the trouble spots. I never would have finished the book without the help of Alex Lapidus, who provided invaluable comments throughout the writing process. The enthusiasm of both gentlemen kept me going. Rafe Sagalyn gave me the optimism I needed to take on such a large project.

Chris DeMuth and David Gerson, the men who make AEI such a special place to work, backed the project from the beginning. Other colleagues, including John Lott, Allan Meltzer, Bruce Kovner, Bob Hahn, Alan Auerbach, Ricardo Caballero, Charlie Calomiris, Tom Hazlett, Larry Lindsey, and John Makin provided many useful suggestions. It was Alan who first suggested to me that a promising connection between Knightian uncertainty and bubbles had been made. Tom suggested the link between bubbles and the California gold rush. Kristie Stokes Hassett morphed from an attorney to an historian, and helped me track down many of the useful details that help tie the book together. Ann Petty provided gifted writing assistance, and Ken Fears and Jessica Pohl worked tirelessly to check every footnote and data item. Harlan Crow provided me with a special place to hide when a week of seclusion was the only thing between me and the last few chapters.

I am especially grateful to John Mahaney of Crown Business for suffering through the first drafts of the manuscript and pointing me in the right direction, and to Shana Wingert for keeping the project on schedule.

Index

About the Author

Kevin A. Hassett is a resident scholar at the American Enterprise Institute who formerly served as a senior economist at the Federal Reserve Board. He received his Ph.D. in economics from the University of Pennsylvania and his B.A. from Swarthmore College.